301

WAYS TO HAVE

FUN

AT WORK

Berrett-Koehler Publishers, Inc.
San Francisco

Berrett-Koehler Publishers, Inc.
450 Sansome Street, Suite 1200
San Francisco, CA 94111-3320
Tel: (415) 288-0260   Fax: (415) 362-2512

ORDERING INFORMATION

Individual sales. Berrett-Koehler publications are available through most bookstores. They can also be ordered direct from Berrett-Koehler at the address above.

Quantity sales. Special discounts are available on quantity purchases by corporations, associations, and others. For details, contact the "Special Sales Department" at the Berrett-Koehler address above.

Orders for college textbook/course adoption use. Please contact Berrett-Koehler Publishers at the address above.

Orders by U.S. trade bookstores and wholesalers. Please contact Publishers Group West, 4065 Hollis Street, Box 8843, Emeryville, CA 94662. Tel: (510) 658-3453; 1-800-788-3123. Fax: (510) 658-1834.

Printed in the United States of America
Printed on acid-free and recycled paper that is composed of 85% recovered fiber, including 15% post-consumer waste.

Library of Congress Cataloging-in-Publication Data
Hemsath, Dave, 1961-
    301 ways to have fun at work / Dave Hemsath & Leslie Yerkes; illustrations by Daniel McQuillen.
      p. cm.
    Includes index.
    ISBN 1-57675-019-1 (alk. paper)
    1. Personnel management. 2. Work environment. 3. Work—Psychological aspects. I. Yerkes, Leslie, 1958- . II. Title.
HF5549.H3928 1997
658.3—dc21

97-10609
CIP

First Edition
99 98 97   10 9 8 7 6 5 4 3 2

Interior Design and Production: Dianne Platner
Copy Editor: Mary Lou Sumberg

To fun-loving people everywhere.

TABLE OF CONTENTS

ACKNOWLEDGMENTS

Dave

T hanks to Jay Schuster who gave me the encouragement to write this book, even though he doesn't know he did it.

Thanks to Laura and Kristen who listen to my kooky ideas, and no thanks to Kristen for "tick tocking" me into doing this one.

Thanks to Berrett-Koehler for taking a chance with us, and a special thanks to Steve and Valerie. Writing this book has been an educational experience for me; I will never look at writing and publishing in the same way again.

Thanks to my wife, Gayle, and my boys, Michael and Derek, who have had to put up with my brutal travel schedule as well as most of my free time being spent on writing this book. You have been patient and supportive, mostly, and I appreciate it. And boys: you finally got your names in a book!

Thanks to my business partner, Patrick, and my coworkers, Lucy, Tom, and Dana. I know that you're laughing at me, not with me.

And a special thanks to Kristen who has been my coach and mentor. This book wouldn't exist if not for your help. Thanks for the ice chips.

T o the team at Berrett-Koehler Publishers for your belief in fun as important, for your willingness to be unconventional in the process of birthing this book, and in recognition of your talent. Thanks for being visionaries.

To my partner in crime, Dave, for pursuing an idea and making fun of me even in my most insane moments. Thanks for being a catalyst.

To Megan for believing in the book and bringing your spirit of fun into our lives. Thanks for being an architect.

To my mother and father for your unconditional love and support, which sustains my spirit for fun. Thanks for being risk takers with me.

To all those fun-loving individuals in workplaces across the nation who generously shared their ideas with us and now with you, the readers. Thanks for being fun.

The secret to having fun in life is to surround yourself with fun people. My love and appreciation to all of my friends, family, and colleagues who make fun with and of me, keeping my life filled with laughter and joy, and particularly to Preston for his steadfast friendship. Thank you for being my teachers, for helping me learn how to lighten up! Why carry a heavy load through life when it isn't necessary?

Leslie

INTRODUCTION

Fun at work—is it an oxymoron or the newest business management trend?

We believe that fun at work may be the single most important trait of a highly effective and successful organization; we see a direct link between fun at work and employee creativity, productivity, morale, satisfaction, and retention, as well as customer service and many other factors that determine business success.

We wanted to help people see that link, so we decided to conduct an international survey to collect real and relevant stories of what actual businesspeople are doing to create fun workplaces. The results have been phenomenal. We received responses from individuals at many levels of the corporate hierarchy, who work within companies of all sizes and in a wide variety of industries. The responses revealed that many successful companies have made fun an integral part of their corporate culture. Fun has become an organizational strategy—a strategic weapon to achieve extraordinary results in areas of corporate life ranging from training sessions to meetings to hiring practices.

Humor consultant and bestselling author C. W. Metcalf wrote in *HR Focus* (February 1993) that "humor is a vital, critical element for human survival, and we often forget about it, and set it aside. We are told that laughter, fun, and play are unadult, unintelligent, and nonprofessional. Nothing could be further from the truth. One of the first indicators of the onset of most mental illness is a loss of the sense of joy in being alive."

Fun and humor help individuals through crisis and change. Because they facilitate the release of tension, fun and humor increase employees' ability to cope with stress on the job and to remain flexible, creative, and innovative under pressure—central features of a strong, resilient corporate culture.

Organizations that integrate fun into work have lower levels of absenteeism, greater job satisfaction, increased productivity, and less downtime. As cited in *HR Focus* in February 1993:

▼ In the nine months that followed a workshop conducted by C. W. Metcalf at Digital Equipment Corporation in Colorado Springs, twenty middle managers increased their productivity by 15 percent and reduced their sick days by half.

▼ Employees from the Colorado Health Sciences Center in Denver who viewed humorous training films and attended fun workshops showed a 25 percent decrease in downtime and a 60 percent increase in job satisfaction.

Fun and the energy it creates are contagious. By far, the most intriguing part of the hundreds of surveys we received are the many stories of the ways that individuals and companies incorporate fun into the workplace.

This book is essentially a compilation of these fun and inspiring stories.

HOW TO USE THIS BOOK

We wrote *301 Ways to Have Fun at Work* for everyone who works: from line employees to managers, from contract workers to senior executives. The book is designed so that you can open it to any page and find valuable ideas to use immediately.

We have organized the book into seven sections to facilitate your finding a fun idea to suit your particular work situation or need. At the end of each section, we present an in-depth case study, which we call a "Fun Focus," that illustrates the theme of the section. The sections are as follows:

work **Work Environment: Giggle While You Work**

communication **Communication: Funny You Should Say That**

training **Training: Learning the Fun-damentals**

meetings **Meetings: Having Fun—Wish You Were Here**

recognition **Recognition: Say It with Fun**

teams **Team Building: How to Create Fun-atics**

acts **Simple Acts of Fun**

Look for the Fun Icons throughout the book, which identify

Fun Facts,

Fun Resources,

and Fun Quotes.

There are even Dave and Leslie Icons, which identify stories we are telling or retelling.

In addition, we have included our Twelve-Step Method to Fun, a program we suggest you share with your coworkers, and follow by implementing one step a month for a year.

At the end of the book is our list of suggested readings—books we highly recommend for your reading pleasure and to aid you in your pursuit of fun at work.

WORK ENVIRONMENT

GIGGLE WHILE YOU WORK

GIGGLE WHILE YOU WORK

the phrase "a fun workplace" doesn't have to be an oxymoron. Anyone can choose to create a fun workplace. Both qualitative and quantitative data exist to support our belief that a fun work environment can have a positive impact on productivity, quality, customer service, and job satisfaction. But still it is a choice that each of us makes.

To infuse your work environment with a spirit of fun, you must value fun as important, you must believe fun to be *essential*.

If you want fun to seep into the fabric of your company culture, start with yourself:

▼ make a conscious effort to lighten up,

▼ plan for fun,

▼ respond spontaneously to fun moments, and

▼ embrace fun as the chosen tone **for** your work environment.

An organization's work environment is both tangible and intangible. It consists of the physical structure of your operation as well as the tone that is set within its walls. It might seem difficult to get a handle on the tone of your environment. It is, however, a real thing and can have tremendous impact on your work .

a n environment that fosters fun is characterized by positive energy, high self-esteem, and team spirit. People feel alive and want to give their best effort to the task. Fun contributes to the creation of an environment that nurtures and sustains what we call employee "want to." You cannot put a price on "want to." Individuals can be trained to do just about anything, but first they must have the motivation. Fun can enhance motivation. If work and the work environment are fun, the results will be better.

To support your pursuit of a **fun** **workplace** and your quest for an enlivened workforce, we will share with you stories, facts, ideas, and resources to stimulate your fun juices for creating your own "Fun Company."

Ask yourself the question each day, "Are we having fun yet?"

▼　▼　▼

Weather can influence attitude in both a positive and a negative way. I know that I prefer clear skies and sunshine. I am happiest and most productive during the long days of summer, when the sun comes up early and stays up late. Recently, as the seasons began to change, our city experienced a week of dark and rainy days that sent my spirits sagging. One morning during this week, determined not to let the weather affect my attitude, I burst into song.

 I serenaded the office with a complete rendition of "The Sun Will Come Out Tomorrow" from the musical *Annie*.

It made me feel better and it was received with laughter. So encouraged was I by the response that I proceeded through the lobby of our office building in full tune, stopping to sing my merry melody to the security guard and the post person. I was chased back to my office with friendly jeers and robust cheers. There is something to be said for carrying a happy tune.

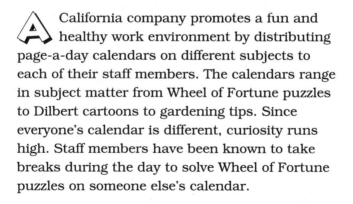

▼　　▼　　▼

A California company promotes a fun and healthy work environment by distributing page-a-day calendars on different subjects to each of their staff members. The calendars range in subject matter from Wheel of Fortune puzzles to Dilbert cartoons to gardening tips. Since everyone's calendar is different, curiosity runs high. Staff members have been known to take breaks during the day to solve Wheel of Fortune puzzles on someone else's calendar.

work

M any businesses are promoting a fun and flexible work environment by implementing a shortened work week during slow times of the year. One San Francisco–based company has summer work hours, closing the office at 1:00 p.m. on Fridays from Memorial Day to Labor Day. The free afternoon may be a time when staff members go to a movie together or just have the freedom to get a head start on their weekend.

"The brain is a wonderful organ. It starts working the moment you get up in the morning and does not stop until you get to the office."

—Robert Frost

F ind a way to symbolize your fun. Trowby Brockman, an insurance industry professional, and her team adopted a mascot— one of those icky, soft rubber toy gorillas. He was affectionately called Gordy. Gordy would show up

fun

in unusual places, particularly when individuals were having a rough day.

During one hurried flight to the home office, Trowby reached into her raincoat pocket to find Gordy. It put a smile on Trowby's face and reminded her that she was traveling with the support and good feelings of the team.

When she was transferred to another office, Trowby continued to benefit from the loyalty of Gordy and her team, who remembered to send occasional cards and good wishes. You never know where Gordy will turn up.

▼   ▼   ▼

T aking one's self too seriously can be deadly. Tom Ziska realized that his workplace, an architecture firm, had become far too serious and stressful, which can be detrimental to the creative nature of the work. Tom went searching for

work

something that would allow people to vent their
frustrations in a healthy and humorous way. He
surprised the office with a pair of parakeets. They
are named after two famous architects—Le
Corbusier and Frank Lloyd Wright. Tom says
about his feathered friends: "Their daily chatter
and presence has done the trick. We give them
the run of the office. To date, no one has
complained about their little 'presents.' When
things get heavy or trying, we ask them what they
would do. It's surprising how often they have
good answers."

T ake advantage of every opportunity
to have fun.

Many nonprofit organizations use
the fundraising strategy
affectionately known as "jail
and bail." Individuals are
sent to "jail" for a couple of
hours. During their

fun

incarceration, the "convicts" are required to raise donations by soliciting "bail" from friends and coworkers. When a community nonprofit organization created a "lock-up," Jerry Kaminski seized the chance to have some fun with his bosses: he sent them to jail for an afternoon. Not only did it become fun for the entire workplace but it also raised money for an important community cause.

A survey of business school deans and business executives revealed that humor plays a significant part in the operation of a healthy, successful business. FACTS

▼ ▼ ▼

Having fun is being prepared to break out of the box—in small ways as well as large. It is doing the unexpected, being willing to look foolish or silly: like singing out loud, or

work

cultivating funny voices, or bowling in the hallway with beach balls and empty boxes. When you take a chance, you break the tension and facilitate an atmosphere of acceptance, freedom, and trust.

ake a list of all the people and things that bring you joy, satisfaction, pleasure, fulfillment, and fun. Refer to it when you are bored, upset, or just need a break. Joy lists are great to exchange with others, too!

Many offices liven up their surroundings with Koosh Balls, the rubbery, stringy balls that are fun to play with and toss around. One of the more popular Koosh toys is the Koosh Basketball— perfect for the back of any office door. For

fun

information regarding Koosh toys, call 800-75-KOOSH. To view a few of the Koosh toys as well as a fun array of other toys and gifts, visit the Kitty Hawk Kites web site at www.kittyhawk.com.

▼   ▼   ▼

W hen our office (like many offices) is stuck with doing a mundane, repetitive job, we often lighten up the atmosphere by listening to music. Occasionally, the local radio station will play an hour or an afternoon of "one-hit wonders," rock groups or singers who only made one memorable song. When a new song comes on, everyone in the office will try to be the first to identify the obscure artist. It doesn't sound like much, but in our small, competitive office an afternoon can soar by as we all attempt to be first to yell out "Video Killed the Radio Star! by the Buggles."

Harmless practical jokes can be a memorable way to create fun in an office. Here is a story of what happened at Printing Industries of America, according to *Association Management* magazine (October 1993).

On July 8, the building manager distributed a routine memo: "This weekend the vendor who installed the cabling in our building will thoroughly clean all of our telephone lines by injecting compressed air into the cables. To control dust and debris that may emanate from your telephone receivers, all staff members are urged to store their telephones in their wastebaskets or to procure special bags from the production department before leaving work on Friday, July 10." More than half the staff asked for the special bags, and the building manager had to get some clear trash can liners to distribute. One woman forgot to procure a bag, worried all weekend, and tried to reach the building manager at home. Over the weekend, the "Mirth Committee" tossed glitter and electrical wire odds and ends into everyone's telephone bag. On Monday morning the staff finally got the message: It was a joke!

fun

ccording to Polly LaBarre in the February 5, 1996, issue of *Industry Week,* Hal Rosenbluth, CEO of Rosenbluth International says, "The only way for us to continuously provide solutions to the needs of an ever-changing business world is to have the kind of environment where spontaneity thrives." One way Hal measures his organization's "happy quotient" is by sending out crayons and a blank piece of paper to employees, who draw their current view of the company. He actually compares these drawings every six months to measure any changes in the way people feel about the company.

▼   ▼   ▼

"A fun work environment allows you to express yourself freely in an appropriate way that generates a feeling of comfort and association among fellow employees."
—Fabian De Rozario, Donaghey Student Center, University of Arkansas, Little Rock

work

T imothy Schrllhardt writes in the October 2, 1996, *Wall Street Journal* that many companies are implementing programs to reduce stress on the job. One of our favorites is that of S. C. Johnson & Son in Racine, Wisconsin. The company subsidizes in-house back and shoulder massages in order to help reduce stress among its forty-three customer service department staffers. Corporate massages have become very popular. For example, Barbara Neims, of Manchester, Connecticut, started a massage service aimed at corporate customers six years ago and has since added six massage therapists to serve her growing client list.

J. David Lewis's office in San Francisco believes that it pays to spend a little money on fun and has come up with the following ideas:
▼ Put up funny art in the office and change it when it gets stale.
▼ Take everyone out to lunch once a month.
▼ Provide candy at meetings.

fun

- ▼ Make sure there is plenty of light in the office. (The "jail look" doesn't facilitate a productive workplace.)
- ▼ Wear casual dress on Friday.
- ▼ Work more hours during the week so there is time for a party on Friday afternoon.
- ▼ Give out mock award certificates for funny things like "Best Hair Day."
- ▼ Pay for everyone to go to a conference once a year.

David writes, "Perhaps the biggest factor in creating fun in the workplace is organization. If everybody is always overworked or behind, they will be stressed out. I think management needs to set realistic production goals and provide competent direction, as well as the resources to support achievement of the goals. Given this structure, even the most challenging work can be fun and not stressful."

work

osie Kramer of the Cleveland Public Schools Adult Education Department told us the story of a friend who collects all types of hats—baseball, fishing, beach, Sunday best. She brought them to work one day and left them tacked to the wall by the coffee station. She posted a sign that said, "Take one and try wearing someone else's hat for a day." It set a great tone that day and created lively conversation.

▼   ▼   ▼

oann Dixon of the Women's Institute for Leadership Development believes strongly in not taking things too seriously. She has shared her philosophy within her organization and they have adopted a "Live Fearlessly" attitude. They support their beliefs with a full-day training workshop in which they practice dealing with difficulties in a resilient manner. They say, "If no

fun

one is going to die, 'it' can't be all that serious."
They feel this helps to take the threat out of any
situation and allows individuals the freedom to
think and to find positive solutions.

▼   ▼   ▼

T ina Laslo of Avery Dennison in Hamilton,
Ohio, wrote that the company installed a
basketball hoop in their parking lot and started a
tournament for employees during lunch break.
For an investment of less than one hundred
dollars, employees had a great way to interact
and to blow off steam.

▼   ▼   ▼

**"Humor is a spontaneous, wonderful bit of an
outburst that just comes. It's unbridled, it's
unplanned, it's full of surprises."**

—Erma Bombeck

work

J ames Mathers, executive vice president of Phillip Day Maddock, believes that while income is certainly a driving force in many successful organizations, happiness is also a front-runner. He says, "You can have happy employees without depleting the organization's coveted bottom line. People who realize that it is okay to laugh a little, joke a little, and actually have fun with the daily grind are not always looking for the cash reward."

▼   ▼   ▼

M ake fun part of your company values.

Cohen and Company, an accounting firm dedicated to the special needs of smaller and growing enterprises, believes that their success stems from their core values. They believe strongly that the secret of their success and well-being lies in an adherence to the values of service, quality, innovation, and fun! Every employee is coached in the values and proudly wears a lapel pin with the acronym SQIF. They have dared to be different in a most serious industry.

fun

FACTS

▼   ▼   ▼

Angela Wiley of the Blonder Company reports that the order department at Blonder plays bingo at least once a week. It's not just regular bingo, however, it's Blonder's Bingo! The Blonder Bingo card consists of a series of customer account numbers, shipping vias, book names, and other company terminology.

Like regular Bingo, the object of the game is to X items vertically, horizontally, or diagonally to win. An order rep must be available to take incoming customer calls in order to play and in order to win. The fun thing about this game is

work

that more than one person can win. Prizes include gift certificates to local restaurants, lunch or breakfast with a supervisor, Blonder logo products, and other fun items.

The order department's customer hold time has improved by 20 percent and the customer abandonment rate by 50 percent on Blonder Bingo days.

▼   ▼   ▼

As a people-oriented company, CDA Management Consulting, Inc., believes that children will have a positive attitude toward work and toward working parents if work is a fun place to be. CDA is a consulting firm that specializes in maximizing the performance of its clients' most valuable and often most expensive asset, its people, and this is reflected in two of its well-known practices.

Children and Babies Welcome. Like most companies, CDA has a no-solicitation policy, but vendors, clients, and guests know that children and babies are always welcome. When a child arrives on site, work stops to give the child a welcome. Toys appear, and for the more precocious, a trip on the Internet is offered. Bobby, one of the more frequent visitors (the vice president's son) has mastered signing on to the computer, getting to the Internet, and finding the latest scoop on *Goosebumps* by popular children's author R. L. Stine.

Family Friendly Week. One week each summer, and usually over one holiday, CDA closes its doors so that the staff can spend time with their families. Voice mail tells callers that the company is closed for appointments, site visits, and training sessions due to Family Friendly Week and that all calls will be returned. Carolyn Pizzuto, the company president, reports that amazingly enough, most callers say their messages can wait and enthusiastically support this fun tradition.

Chuck Behrens of New Life Hospice uses voice mail to surprise people with an unexpected dose of fun. Take advantage of the opportunity to brighten another person's day with a message that conveys a spirit of fun while facilitating the exchange of information. This unanticipated event will make the call memorable.

▼   ▼   ▼

Allow and even encourage individuals to create a positive working atmosphere at their desks with photos and fun toys. Today, so many companies are idea-based that an atmosphere of fun helps to bring out fresh ideas and keep people out of ruts. Some of the more popular toys are hula hoops (used at Organic Online in San Francisco); Legos, Nerf guns, Pez dispensers (Oracle Corp.); pogo sticks, Frisbees, sandboxes (Oracle, again); foosball and Silly Putty (Netscape).

fun

"We are under a lot of pressure, and toys are our comfort. We need them like Linus needs his blanket."

—Mary Owen, Oracle Corp., quoted by Mark Leibovich in the "San Jose Mercury News," August 4, 1996

▼　　▼　　▼

G oofing around can help reduce the pressure of high-stress jobs. Organized goofing around can help build team spirit and foster creativity. Spontaneous contests like relay races in office chairs (wheels on the chairs preferred), marshmallow fights, and team Nerf gun fights help break up a workday and allow everyone to bring a renewed spirit to their work.

▼　　▼　　▼

T he Wall Street environment in New York can be very fast paced and stressful. Yael Zofi of J. P. Morgan has found that fun can increase

work

teamwork and improve the quality of work. For example, playing Pictionary at lunch is a great way to give your coworkers a fun, creative outlet that makes the day go faster. Games tend to be a great tension reliever.

▼   ▼   ▼

Eileen Douse of Human Dynamics knows how her energy level and that of her coworkers drops in the middle of the afternoon on most workdays. In an effort to reenergize herself and stir her creative juices, Eileen started an office ritual called "the wacky hour." Every day at 3:00 p.m., Eileen and her office mate spin wildly in their office chairs for thirty seconds. At the end of thirty seconds, they return to whatever work they were doing. They have found that even a short break of doing something physical and foolish helps revive them when the afternoon doldrums begin.

fun

24

"A few minutes of fun can do wonders for stress. When stress is lower, quality and productivity improve. When quality and productivity are high and stress is low, this will lead to job satisfaction and low turnover rates."

—Phyllis Van, Organizational Effectiveness Specialist, Rockwell-Collins Businesses

▼ ▼ ▼

Matilda Reeder, training manager at SABRE Decision Technologies, was not into New Year's resolutions, but she felt drastic measures were in order to stop a personal habit. Enlisting the help of her staff and coworkers, Matilda started the new year with a "cussing jar." Every time she uttered a profanity, she added twenty-five cents to the jar. The idea became popular and others joined in to make donations for each slip of the lip. Other departments soon set up their own "sin tax" collection jars for violations in meeting attendance, missed deadlines, and so on. The proceeds were used for office get-togethers and especially for morning donuts.

work

Faith Popcorn, in her bestselling books *The Popcorn Report* and *Clicking,* describes a trend in society that she calls "99 Lives." She loosely defines 99 Lives as "the idea that we have too little time, too many responsibilities, and not enough of ourselves to spread around." In response to this increasing demand on our time, some companies have taken to instituting a companywide Quiet Time. According to Popcorn, "Every workday, between the hours of 10 and 11 a.m., all phones are turned off and messages routed to voice mail. The fax and copy machine are unplugged. Quiet Time has become the most productive time of the day."

▼　　▼　　▼

Rebecca Rogers at University Hospitals in Augusta, Georgia, has developed a fun activity that she calls "communal captions." To while away spare time at the copy machine, she posts photos from newspapers and magazines and invites staff members to write funny captions on a blank piece of paper beneath the picture. Sometimes puzzles, games, or riddles are posted to challenge copy machine users.

fun

Many organizations thrive on the cartoon antics of Dilbert, the character created by Scott Adams. For anyone who is unfamiliar with Dilbert or does not get the comic strip in their local paper, two compilations of Adam's work, "Fugitive from the Cubicle Police" and "Still Pumped from Using the Mouse," have recently been published. These books should give your office hours of chuckles.

▼　　▼　　▼

Western Wireless Corporation operates a customer service call center that is open 24 hours a day, 7 days a week, 365 days a year. The company recognizes that employees at the call center handle a high volume of work that requires them to be consistently diplomatic and positive. Because of the stressful nature of the work, the company encourages activities to boost morale.

Stephanie Dropping, professional development manager for Western Wireless, participates in a customer service "spirit

work

committee" formed by her company. The committee has organized various fun activities, including a customer service Olympics. The Olympics featured sports and job-related events. Individuals were awarded bronze, silver, and gold medals for their achievements. The goal of the committee was to have everyone be a winner.

When asked why it is important to spend time on fun activities, Stephanie replied quickly that "the objective is to reduce the stress of the job and keep the human element in the work."

▼   ▼   ▼

Eastman Kodak Company takes advantage of making every day an exciting day. To spice up the work week, the company hosts such events as Pig Outs, Friday Donut Breakfasts, Casual Day, and Halloween Costume Contests.

fun

Capital One Services of Tampa, Florida, is very serious about creating a fun office environment. According to Inette Dishler, the company has developed employee-driven "scream teams" to maintain a fun and positive environment. The teams cover the areas of morale, peer recognition, birthdays/anniversaries, holidays, sports, community involvement, and contests. The scream teams are responsible to develop theme days on which everyone dresses up or brings in food. They also sponsor quarterly morale events like company picnics and Wacky Olympics.

▼　　▼　　▼

Angela Gann, manager of administration and training services for a large health-care company, often decorates her office and uses it as a fun refuge for her coworkers. During a stressful reorganization, Angela covered her door with a large piece of chart paper so people could release their frustration by drawing, scribbling, and venting their feelings. At the same time, her entire wall was covered with paper for people to post their favorite cartoons.

work

Music is a fun tonic. Researchers at the University of Illinois have found that when workers listen to the music of their choice, their productivity improves, whether they are engaged in administrative tasks or more complex analytical work. What's more, tuned-in employees report feeling more enthusiastic and relaxed.

—"San Francisco Examiner"

▼   ▼   ▼

Companies can enliven the workplace by hiring people who are humorous and creative. A willingness to trust and empower these employees may create a fun environment that can increase sales and improve customer service.

According to Bob Filipczak of *Training* magazine (April 1995), Amy Miller, CEO of Amy's Ice Cream in Austin, Texas, was totally unaware that her employees had devised a highly creative solution to a difficult situation. Realizing that service workers can have a bad attitude toward

fun

customers who come into a store right before closing, store managers started a late-night tradition. Instead of being angry at late arrivals and glowering at them until they leave, the employees began lock-ins on Wednesday nights. Customers still in the store at closing time were detained and not allowed to leave until they learned the Time Warp dance from the movie *The Rocky Horror Picture Show*. Instead of frightening customers away, people flocked to the store on Wednesday nights to have an opportunity to be locked in and dance on top of the ice cream coolers. (Amy's Ice Cream was featured in the November 1996 issue of *Inc.* magazine in an article entitled "Corporate Culture.")

▼ ▼ ▼

If you happen to have a long hallway in your office, start a Friday afternoon bowling league. One health services company based in Oakland, California, bought a bowling set to use on their Friday afternoon breaks. They have even been known to award trophies.

Working with people who like what they're doing helps to make the workplace fun. At Fredrickson Communication, managers strive to hire only the best to achieve a fit with the Fredrickson company culture. In the interview, project leaders Sheila Machacek and Terry Brennan discuss how individuals are encouraged to have fun, work reasonable hours, and be creative. They boast that their hiring efforts have been pretty right-on thus far.

▼   ▼   ▼

At Southwest Airlines, new hires are encouraged to view the Southwest memorabilia and history that decorate the hallways at the People University (Southwest's training department) and to pester other employees to fill in the missing details. This is a kind of fill-in-the-blank way of learning about the company and also of meeting new coworkers.

fun

O ffice fun is often a drawing card for ingenious young adults who want to join a high-tech firm. In California, Silicon Valley companies use fun and creativity as a recruiting tool. Several companies promote their zaniness. Sun Microsystems reports on April Fools' Day pranks in their corporate overview, which appears on their World Wide Web site; Berkeley Systems promotes the use of a three and one-half turn slide that connects the second floor to the company kitchen.

▼   ▼   ▼

A ccording to Mark Leibovich in his article "All Work and Some Play" in the August 4, 1996, *San Jose Mercury News,* Silly Putty seems to have several applications in Silicon Valley companies. Jim Gellman, a Netscape engineer, gives prospective job candidates a hunk of Silly Putty when they come to his office just to see how they react. He has been known to take an imprint of an application on a Silly Putty pancake.

work

HealthEast in St. Paul, Minnesota, created a "drop-in" lunch buffet to meet prospective candidates for employment. During a two-hour period, office personnel are asked to drop in for lunch to socialize and interact with potential new hires. They feel this is an excellent way to get to know someone on a more personal basis as well as to see if there is a fit with the other team members.

▼　　▼　　▼

Angela Gann of Kaiser Permanente likes to send a personal note of appreciation to everyone she interviews, except the successful candidate. The successful candidate gets special treatment—for example, a huge "Congratulations" sign draped across their workstation on their first morning at work; or maybe a Halloween jack-o-lantern bucket filled with candy; a fun squishy fish pen; or a headband with either glitter hearts, glitter stars, or glitter balls attached.

fun

DAVE'S (HEMSATH)

TOP TEN LIST

of most popular fun foods for work (as compiled from our surveys). Notice the lack of healthy choices on this list!

10. Beer (champagne, wine)
9. $100, 000 candy bars (great for recognition)
8. Pretzels (to go with the beer?)
7. M&M's (candy in general)
6. Cake
5. Popcorn
4. Ice cream
3. Doughnuts
2. Pizza, and
#1. Cookies (the overwhelming choice)

work

How do you discover if a job candidate is really a fun-loving person? It doesn't take any more effort than following the process you've already developed for hiring peak performers. Just add a few fun touches.

▼ Make sure that a sense of humor is on your list of character and competency criteria for the job.

▼ Rewrite the job description to reflect the skills and attributes of individuals who use fun as a means for being successful.

▼ Take a fun and unconventional approach to finding candidates. Use outrageous words and graphics to attract a more lighthearted yet qualified candidate.

▼ Conduct your interviews in a more informal and fun atmosphere.

▼ Ask situation questions that require the candidate to describe how they managed in different, challenging workplace scenarios.

▼ Involve individuals in the interviewing from the department where the new hire will be working.

▼ Don't be afraid to throw the candidate a curveball, like conducting the interview in Groucho glasses. (Remember to stay within the legal guidelines of questioning.)

fun

- ▼ Ask the candidate about their "ideal" workplace.
- ▼ Ask the candidate to describe to you how they would bring energy to the company and to their work.
- ▼ Propose to the candidate an opportunity to test the job by working at it for a day or two before finally contracting.
- ▼ Of course, maintain your procedures for testing and reference checking.

A process that is fun will attract and retain candidates who feel most comfortable in a work culture where fun is expected.

▼　▼　▼

A survey of one thousand employees ranked their needs in the workplace in order of preference. Their one hundred immediate supervisors were also surveyed and ranked the same needs in order of preference, based on what the supervisors thought their employees would say. Following are the results:

FACTS

work

RANKING THE NEEDS IN THE WORKPLACE	Empolyees	Managers
Interesting work	#1	#5
Full appreciation for work done	2	8
Feeling "in on things"	3	10
Job security	4	2
Good wages	5	1
Promotion/growth opportunities	6	3
Good working conditions	7	4
Personal loyalty to workers	8	6
Tactful disciplining	9	7
Sympathetic help with personal problems	10	9

—Dr. Kenneth Kovach, George Mason University, "People Performance" magazine, October 1996

fun

FUN FOCUS

PROGRESSIVE INSURANCE: OUTRAGEOUS IS OUR MIDDLE NAME

Progressive Insurance is widely regarded as one of the best managed and most profitable insurance companies in America. The company began in Cleveland, Ohio, in 1937 and quickly became a market leader in providing nonstandard auto insurance. Today, Progressive consists of sixty-plus operating subsidiaries that provide auto insurance and other specialty property–casualty insurance and related services to the marketplace. Progressive markets its products primarily through independent insurance agents in the United States and Canada.

As the seventh largest U.S. private passenger auto insurer, Progressive's major product lines include private passenger auto (nonstandard, standard, and preferred) insurance for recreational vehicles and small fleets of commercial vehicles. The company has a 2.8 percent share of the $100 billion market ($20 billion for nonstandard and $80 billion for standard and preferred). In 1995, Progressive's net income was $250 million on $3.01 billion in sales. Progressive actively markets in over forty states, with seven states accounting for over 55 percent of its business. The company employs almost ten thousand people.

work

A WORK HARD/PLAY HARD CULTURE

Progressive has a reputation for attracting and retaining bright, hard-working, and creative people at all levels. The company pushes responsibility down the organizational levels, encourages experimentation, tolerates—and even encourages—mistakes, and rewards people based on results.

Back in 1984, the company first articulated its core values in its annual report. The first version listed three driving forces behind the success of the organization: profit, excellence, and fun. Each year, the statements would be reviewed and modified as the company learned more about itself. While "fun" became a more implicit and less explicit core value in subsequent years, it still remained an important aspect of the culture.

Manifestations of this fun culture are visible everywhere, from the casual work atmosphere that starts with the senior executives, who are rarely seen in traditional business attire, to the famous collection of contemporary art that adds to a creatively stimulating, sometimes provocative or bizarre, and often whimsical workplace. But perhaps the most visible aspect of fun at Progressive occurs every year at the end of October.

A PROGRESSIVE HALLOWEEN

No ones knows when the Halloween tradition actually began at Progressive. It may have started gradually in the mid-seventies when the company moved into its new suburban headquarters. Employees were allowed, actually encouraged, to come to work in costumes. They also decorated their work areas or entire departments. The event quickly spread to major division locations in other states.

fun

40

Many groups spend hours in planning and construction on their own time.

Everyone begins the day by visiting other work areas to admire the imaginative and often outlandish outfits and decorations. Senior managers are included, often surprising coworkers with their creativity and nerve. One year, CEO Peter B. Lewis appeared as the Lone Ranger, another year he was Zorro, and another year he was a swimmer wearing a swimming pool.

Other executives have dressed as cavemen, gangsters, or robots. Going well beyond the typical ghosts, witches, or monsters, employees have shown up as the Wizard of Oz, Peanuts or other cartoon characters, rock stars, a large box of crayons, the crew of the Starship Enterprise, or a six-pack of beer. Each division awards prizes for costumes or unit decorations in various categories. Family members and even vendors make a point of showing up to tour the amazing creativity on display that day. The Cleveland TV program *PM Magazine* even did a feature one year showcasing Progressive's outrageous celebration.

ORGANIZATIONAL DIVIDENDS

Why do employees do this? And more importantly, why does management allow and encourage it and participate so enthusiastically themselves? The answer may be at the core of Progressive's fun culture. "We spend more time at work than anywhere else" said CEO Lewis. "Life's too short not to enjoy one's work. A creatively stimulating and fun work atmosphere enhances individual energy and job satisfaction. People who have more fun at work usually work harder and achieve better results."

work

COMMUNICATION

FUNNY YOU SHOULD SAY THAT

COMMUNICATION

FUNNY YOU
SHOULD SAY
THAT

Not enough. Not accurate. Not timely.

These are the complaints most often
heard when employees discuss corporate
communication . The lack of information can
be a deciding factor in business success or
failure, affecting critical decisions, important
negotiations, and essential relationships.

Jan Carlson, former CEO of Scandinavian
Airlines, says, "An employee not provided with
information will not take responsibility, but an

employee provided with information cannot but take responsibility."

Information is power in the most positive sense. Healthy organizations flood their environments with complete information communicated in a timely fashion. The model **for** "open book" management is being adopted as a more successful approach for cultivating employee involvement and **empowerment**.

It is not only important to share information throughout the organization in an expedient manner but also to deliver the message in a sensitive manner. If you communicate in a fun **and** memorable way, you will grab the attention of your audience, engage their interest, and enliven their willingness to act. Communication is a vital key for **success** in any company.

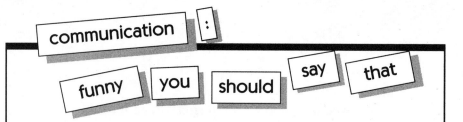
B ring back "handles," those interesting nicknames that CB radio enthusiasts have. Instead of sending a memo to Patrick, send it to "Gumby Jones." Allow people to have alter-ego names on office doors, stationery, or wherever. The next time you redo your voice mail make it, "You have reached the office of Kobra Kabanna . . ." Project leaders can improve their titles. Instead of having a title like Fire Prevention Coordinator, use "Goddess of Fire."

▼   ▼   ▼

I n August 1995, *Agency Sales* magazine reported that a Hughes Aircraft Company (HAC) site recently experienced a slow and chaotic change to a new telephone system. After two weeks, many phones still had no dial tone. One engineer created a sign that parodied the transition from Pac-Bell to the new "HAC-Bell." Copies of the sign were soon posted throughout the plant. The sign

fun

may not have been humorous to an outsider, but it was very funny to those who shared the frustration of working without a phone. Work-related humor, especially when it is shared with coworkers, can diffuse tension and at the same time give a subtle message to management.

"Fax This Book!" is a handy guide to livening up cover letters on your faxes. Published by Workman Publishing, it is available in most bookstores for $10.95.

▼ ▼ ▼

Look for a humorous second meaning in communications with customers or coworkers. Several teachers, insurance claims agents, and even cast members at Disneyland wrote that they compile lists of unintentionally funny statements. In a student's vocabulary assignment, a teacher found the following definition: "An active verb shows action; a passive verb shows passion." A Disneyland cast member was once asked, "At what time is the nine o'clock parade?" One man wrote on his insurance claim form, "After seeing my mother-in-law, I backed into the wall." A collection of nonstandard meanings to everyday events helps keep work in perspective.

▼   ▼   ▼

A good way to stay in communication with your clients is through humor. A young salesman who was eager to secure our business maintained regular contact without becoming pushy or intrusive by sending us humorous quotes, jokes, and stories via the fax machine. His funny missives were passed around the office and frequently forwarded on to other unsuspecting colleagues. The faxes were a pleasant surprise whenever they poured forth from

our friendly fax machine and a nice change from the more mundane communications that we receive daily.

P.S. His efforts did not go unrewarded. When the time was right and the need more pressing, we cemented a business relationship. The glue that bonded his sale was a shared sense of humor.

▼   ▼   ▼

D eliver bad news with an appropriate sense of humor.

Recently several pieces of exercise equipment in a heavily utilized fitness center broke down. While parts were being ordered, a humorous sign was posted on each piece of equipment.

This facility was attacked by screw-eating Martians earlier this week. We waged a good battle, but they succeeded in disabling two of our most popular machines. We are working quickly to secure the premises and repair these machines. Sorry for the inconvenience.

communication

During the time the repairs were being made, there wasn't a single complaint. In fact, there were many patrons who commented in a positive way about the signs.

▼   ▼   ▼

"An employee who makes 'light' of a serious situation makes me say to myself, 'Yeah, it isn't that bad' or, 'It could be a lot worse.'"
—Tom Krupa, Gale's Garden Center

▼   ▼   ▼

Are you frustrated because your coworkers aren't paying attention to the memo you painstakingly prepared to communicate vital information? Spice up your memo with intrigue by sending it under an alias, or even keep the sender anonymous and challenge everyone to guess who it came from. This should get their attention focused on the memo.

fun

C reate a fun suggestion box. Encourage all employees to contribute their suggestions for fun activities.

As reported in the *Cleveland Plain Dealer* (January 16, 1997), Paul Orfalea, founder of Kinko's, believes that Kinko's suggestion box is one of the secrets to their success. The employee who provides the best suggestion each year wins an all-expense-paid trip to Disney World. But what makes it really fun is that everyone who works in that store gets to go along. While the employees are gone, Kinko's top brass fills in for them.

O n Frisbee Memo Day at Pacific Power and Electric in Portland, Oregon, formal memos and messages are delivered throughout the office attached to Frisbees.

communication

$\mathcal{S}$ cott Friedman of Denver, Colorado, believes that "Humor is a form of communication. It is a most useful weapon. A sense of humor is not the ability to tell jokes; a sense of humor is the ability to find something funny in your predicament and to not take yourself so seriously."

"A sense of humor keen enough to show a man his own absurdities, as well as those of other people, will keep him from the commission of all sins, or nearly all, save those that are worth committing."
—Samuel Butler

$\mathcal{M}$ any organizations have a formal internal communication vehicle. At SWI in Naperville, Illinois, management decided to ask employees what fun ideas or thoughts they wanted to include in the weekly employee

fun

newsletter. The response was tremendous, with ideas like the following:

- ▼ reviews of local restaurants,
- ▼ movie reviews,
- ▼ crossword puzzles with employee names,
- ▼ a "what's happening" column with news about employees' lives,
- ▼ jokes, and
- ▼ space for experimental ideas.

The newsletter generated some unexpected results.

1. It raised morale for employees by providing recognition and an opportunity to share and be given credit for ideas.
2. It expressed the notion that "we take our business seriously, but we do not necessarily take ourselves seriously."
3. It gave employees practice in writing skills.
4. It gave everyone at the office something to talk about. ("I saw your daughter made the soccer team!")
5. It gave people something to look forward to every week.
6. The list of movie and restaurant reviews became popular not only with employees but also with clients.

Communicate, communicate, communicate: the cardinal rule of a healthy workplace. Bill Ryan of Master Consulting Group believes that communication should be visible to all. At his company, they track sales progress with a large graphic strategically placed for all to see. The graphic depicts a jogger advancing toward the company goal. In months when the goal is achieved, the jogger is smiling. In months when the goal has been difficult to achieve, the jogger struggles. And if the goal is less than 50 percent achieved, the jogger crashes over a hurdle.

The goal chart generates a lot of interest and motivation. In fact, it resulted in immediate sales growth. Within one month, they went from being two months behind goal to being one and one-half months ahead of goal. Bill Ryan learned that communicating progress against a goal in a manner that is fun and nonthreatening can work wonders.

GOAL

fun

"When fun is part of your culture, people are more relaxed and open to thinking about new, creative, or innovative ideas—a trait that always has been and always will be a competitive advantage."

—Cathy Miller, PacifiCorp

▼ ▼ ▼

A smile can have a positive effect on the sound of your voice. People will generally respond more favorably to you if you smile while talking to them. The sales manager from a small manufacturer in Toledo, Ohio, knows that smiles not only work in person but also over the telephone lines. As a constant reminder of the importance of smiling, he has large-lettered the word *SMILE* on a piece of paper and attached it to the handset of his telephone. Now, every time he picks up the phone to talk to a customer, his voice has a smile in it.

He has also put a mirror next to his phone so that when he is talking he can look at his smiling reflection, which of course keeps him grinning.

communication

As reported in *USA Today* on November 11, 1996, Southwest Airlines feels that streamlining communications is one of the keys to their success. They feel poor communication creates complexity and confusion. Southwest keeps their employees fully informed through the company newsletter, *LUV Lines*. Industry news, route information, baggage handling and arrival statistics, virtually every facet of the company is openly discussed. Southwest believes that when employees have immediate access to critical information, they can make the necessary adjustments to fix problems more quickly.

"Happy employees care more for quality and outcome. They create an atmosphere that reduces conflict and turnover, which makes customers satisfied and happy."

—Abe Bakhsheshy, Director of Customer Service, University of Utah Hospital

fun

S ome organizations have started underground, in-house chat groups that converse via email—a sort of cyber gossip. Although it may sound subversive, it is a great way to discuss the latest company policy, to vent about a frustrating customer, or to issue fashion citations to employees who have been observed committing major fashion errors. A perfect substitute for water-cooler conversations.

Elaine Henna, quality coordinator at MAMTC in Wichita, Kansas, has found that email is a great tool for sharing a joke-of-the-day with her colleagues.

Creativity and fun go hand in hand. Bradley Wilkinson, of Bradleylew, Inc., in Atlanta, likes to improvise interoffice memos by trying to create a poem for each written communication. It might seem like a challenge for those of us who are uncomfortable writing, but what a great way to get people to actually look forward to receiving one of your memos. "Roses are Red . . ."

Research has pointed out that people with a well-developed sense of humor are not only more at ease with themselves, they are happier and more productive in everything they do. Humor is a valuable resource that is available to everyone at any age. It relieves tension and stress. It brings groups of people closer together. When used in the workplace, humor can increase productivity, improve communication, and enhance employee morale.

—"Agency Sales" magazine, August 1995

fun

mail and voice mail are becoming the primary way people communicate these days. In order to make it more entertaining, Judy Beam, an instructor at Western Michigan University in Kalamazoo, leaves her messages in character—specifically historical character. How interesting to receive voice mail form Abraham Lincoln, "Four score and seven years ago, your paper was due." Well, it might not be that interesting from a student's perspective.

To build on this idea, you could leave messages from characters who inhabit literature, television, or movies. It might be fun to have a cast of characters to draw from, depending on the type of message you are leaving. "Dick Tracy" could be investigating why your phone calls are not being returned, and "Lieutenant Data" from the Starship Enterprise might call with the information you requested.

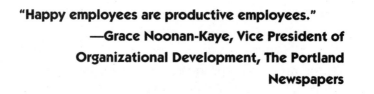

"Happy employees are productive employees."
—Grace Noonan-Kaye, Vice President of
Organizational Development, The Portland
Newspapers

▼   ▼   ▼

Michael Blaszak from Sandusky, Ohio, has devised a clever way for his staff to keep on their toes while speaking with clients on the phone. Each morning, everyone chips in one dollar to an office pool. An employee wins that day's pool if they use the "phrase of the day" most often in the course of normal conversation with their customers. Sample phrases are: "Rome wasn't built in a day," or "It's easier to get a camel through the eye of a needle," or "To err is human." Sometimes an obscure word is substituted for the phrase of the day. The result is a staff that stays sharp, even though they may be on the phone all day.

fun

If you run a telemarketing or customer service department, you know that it can be difficult for your clients to remember who their sales rep is. Kevin Ferlin of Logan Marketing in Cleveland, Ohio, has come up with a fun way to keep clients communicating with the right sales rep. Each rep is given a first name to coincide with the territory they service. Abigail covers Alaska and Alabama while Karen handles Kansas and Kentucky. If a customers calls in and doesn't know who their rep is, all they need to do is mention where they are calling from.

TONY

▼   ▼   ▼

Email has become a serious vehicle for fun. In many offices, the daily Dilbert cartoon is the extent of the circulated office humor. In the Office of Staff Development for the St. Vrain Valley School District in Colorado, email is used to circulate the David Letterman Top Ten List. Check your local paper; in many cities, the Top Ten List is printed the next morning. To personalize the list for your own office try adding an eleventh or twelfth idea to Dave's list.

For example, here are Dave Hemsath's Top Ten Ways People Have Fun at Work (based on my unscientific estimates of how often people gave these responses in our surveys).

DAVE'S (HEMSATH)

TOP TEN LIST

10. **Dance the Macarena**
9. **Group outing (lunch, dinner, or happy hour)**
8. **Celebrate birthdays and anniversaries**
7. **Post cartoons (Dilbert) on doors, bulletin boards, etc.**
6. **Dress up on Halloween**
5. **Have a positive attitude**
4. **Casual dress Friday**
3. **Tell jokes**
2. **Eat (foods vary), and**
#1. **SMILE**

fun

The Bonneville Power Administration in Portland, Oregon, began a weekly newsletter for a colleague who had been taken ill. They had so much fun writing and reading what others had written that they continued the practice after their coworker returned to work. This is a nice, informal way to keep up with what is going on in everyone's life.

▼   ▼   ▼

"We feel a fun atmosphere builds a strong sense of community. It also counterbalances the stress of hard work and competition."
—Elizabeth Pedrick Sartain, Southwest Airlines

▼   ▼   ▼

Turina Bakken, director of programs for MAQIN in Madison, Wisconsin, uses an updated version of mood rings as a form of office communication. Turina writes:

"We each have a color wheel at our desk that looks like a board game spinner. We paste funny pictures in the sections to let each other know how we are feeling on that day. Since we work in an open environment, it acts like a 'door' to let people know if you want to be interrupted or not. It's a very light and informal way to respect each other's privacy and state of mind. Basically, red means off limits, yellow means proceed with caution, and green means come on in. Each person makes up their own funny key to what the colors mean to them."

Roger von Oech, author of the books "A Whack on the Side of the Head" and "A Kick in the Seat of the Pants," has a series of small cards that he calls "Creative Whacks." These little cards can be distributed to meeting participants to help spur creative thinking when a meeting becomes bogged down. For more information on "Creative Whacks" and some of Roger's other creative thinking products, call 415-321-6775.

fun

64

C orporate documents are some of the most basic and boring forms of office communication. Try to inject some fun into these mundane documents. Here is what one company did with their employment application.

Bob Filipczak reports in the April 1995 issue of *Training* magazine that at Amy's Ice Cream in Austin, Texas, all you get for an employment application is a paper bag. You're asked to do something creative with it while including at least your name and phone number. They have received several unique applications. One bag came back attached to a helium balloon, made to look like the basket of a hot-air balloon. The basket had pictures of the applicant's accomplishments as well as other items that were significant to the person. Another applicant converted the bag into a makeshift aquarium, complete with live goldfish.

FUN FOCUS

organization knows how to enliven and energize their very unique workplace.

ABOUT THE ROCK AND ROLL HALL OF FAME

GIRLS (AND BOYS) JUST WANT TO HAVE FUN AT THE ROCK AND ROLL HALL OF FAME

The Rock and Roll Hall of Fame is not your typical workplace. It exists to honor the vibrant, dynamic, even crazy music called rock and roll. The Rock Hall is not big on specific fun activities, but has developed a culture that mirrors the art they preserve. From the psychedelic forklift truck to "chef of the day" staff meetings, this

The Rock and Roll Hall of Fame and Museum (RRHFM) is a 150,000-square-foot facility that serves as the home of rock and roll's vital heritage, providing dynamic interactive exhibits, performance spaces, special programs, and displays from the museum's permanent collection. Most importantly, it is the "permanent home" of the one hundred or so artists and nonperformers who have been inducted into its Hall of Fame.

The concept of a Rock and Roll Hall of Fame was initiated in 1983 when a group of influential personalities in the music industry created the Rock and Roll Hall of Fame Foundation to honor the men and women who have made

fun

unique contributions to the energy and evolution of rock and roll. In 1986, after a nationwide search for an appropriate location, Cleveland, Ohio, was selected. The state of the art facility was designed by internationally renowned architect I. M. Pei and built on the shores of Lake Erie in downtown Cleveland.

The Rock Hall officially opened in September of 1995 and has been a tremendous success. Attendance the first year ran 25 percent above expectations. Visitors have come from every state in the union and from over sixty foreign countries. In August of 1996, the Hall greeted its one millionth guest. The Rock Hall, now entering its second full year of operation, expects to exceed attendance projections again, and has set a goal to have 40 percent or more of the Hall's visitors return for a second or third visit.

THE CULTURE CLUB

Within a short period of time, the RRHFM has developed a unique culture of open communication throughout the entire organization. From CEO William Hulett's staffwide meetings and social gatherings, down to department-level staff meetings in the homes of the department directors (a different staff member is required to cook and serve breakfast to their coworkers each week), there is a free flow of communication throughout the Hall.

The openness of the building's architecture is carried over to an openness among the different departments. For example, a typical orientation for a new hire involves spending two to three days learning what each department does and why they do it. In addition, a good deal of time is spent learning about the Rock Hall's history, how the project was developed, and

communication

the physical aspects of the facility. By the end of orientation, new hires feel as if they have become part of something bigger than themselves, specifically they feel as if they have become part of a family. RRHFM staff members gain a sense of ownership and pride in the organization they represent. This is extremely important to an organization whose sole purpose is to share their work with the world.

THE HEART OF ROCK AND ROLL

While the word "fun" may not appear on the Rock Hall's mission statement, by the very nature of its subject matter, the Hall tends to be a light-hearted, exciting place to work. Spontaneous singing and dancing are daily occurrences for museum staffers—no Muzak in this workplace.

As a way of acknowledging that serious work must be accomplished during museum hours, however, the Rock Hall recognizes its employees in special ways. For example, it has become a tradition to hold monthly after-hours birthday parties for all employees who have a birthday that month. All staff members are encouraged, but not required, to attend these celebrations. Another tradition honors an employee's first anniversary of work at the Hall by allowing them to sign and date the psychedelic mural painted on the wall of the employee entrance.

Fun is an accepted and encouraged part of the Rock Hall culture. "A Rock and Roll Hall of Fame could not exist if it were not a fun place to work," says Tim Moore, director of communications. "If our employees were not having fun, we would not be reflecting what rock music is all about."

TRAINING

LEARNING THE FUN-DAMENTALS

LEARNING THE FUN-DAMENTALS

Productivity is a performance art. The individual who performs well succeeds. When people are energized, they perform. When people are having fun, they are energized. So **fun** is clearly a formula for success.

It is the goal of all trainers to facilitate **learning** —to help people discover and utilize their talents as well as to develop and practice the skills and habits essential to their success; to increase the productive capacity of individuals and teams working within an organization; to facilitate productive responses by employees to changing company needs; and above all to motivate and energize people so they want to learn and improve their skills.

Fun **is** an important tool in the toolbox of any trainer. As humor consultant C. W. Metcalf says, "Plug it in, and it works." Infuse your training with acts of fun and you will engage your audience. Fun is an integral element of adult learning. Fun will make your training **memorable** . Fun will facilitate lasting effects. And fun will keep them coming back for more!

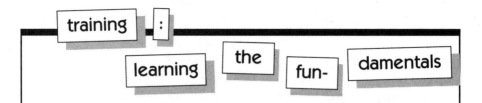

R obert Marn of the Chilcote Company tackled a serious problem with a fun solution. The organization was experiencing an increase in their workers' compensation premiums and job-related injuries. In 1995, the company instituted a safety bingo game. Learning became fun and the accidents decreased by a rate of 56 percent from the previous year. The impact was significant, with a 55 percent drop in lost time equating to thirty-eight days of work and a savings of $21,000.00 in workers' compensation premiums. Wow!

J ump start your organization's fun by hiring a humor consultant. Sometimes an outside expert provides a fresh perspective.

There are many great fun and humor consultants who can help enliven your workplace. Following are a few to investigate if your company is interested:

The Humor Project
Dr. Joel Goodman
110 Spring Street
Saratoga Springs, NY 12866
Phone: 518-587-8770

Playfair Inc.
Matt Weinstein
2207 Oregon Street
Berkeley, CA 94705
Phone: 510-540-8768

Funny Business Inc.
Dr. Steve Allen
8 Labrand Court
Ithaca, NY 14850
Phone: 607-277-1695

Humor Consultants Inc.
Phil Sorentino
1631 Northwest Professional Plaza, Suite 107
Columbus, OH 43220
Phone: 614-451-5390

ccording to the August 1995 issue of *Agency Sales* magazine, you can teach employees how to do a task by exaggerating how not to perform the task. When presented with a ridiculously bad example, employees can learn both "how to" and "how not to" do a job.

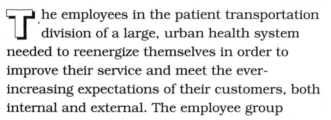

The employees in the patient transportation division of a large, urban health system needed to reenergize themselves in order to improve their service and meet the ever-increasing expectations of their customers, both internal and external. The employee group created a vision for their improvement effort. The vision included the development of performance standards, customer service training, a reengineered system for dispatch, and even an overhaul of their dress code.

fun

The group decided to have some fun with the selection of a new uniform. They invited all patient transportation employees to a breakfast that boasted a sumptuous buffet and festive decorations. During the meeting, employees were dazzled by a fashion show featuring possible uniform choices, modeled by their peers who strutted their stuff down a runway stage with music to accompany their stroll. All members of the department then cast their vote for the uniform they preferred.

This effort to include all employees in the decision and have fun with the selection of uniforms fostered a renewed sense of esprit de corps within the group and facilitated a smooth transition between uniforms. It was also a lot of fun!

"Fun in the workplace is being able to interject something that is entertaining while still accomplishing your work responsibilities."
—Joe Mullenax, Hoechst Celanese Chemical Group

training

▼ ▼ ▼

Transfer fun from one setting to another. Bring fun rituals that you enjoy from another environment into the workplace. For example, the wave, a ritual in which thousands of individuals participate in ballparks across the nation, is fun to insert into a company training. Can you think of any others?

fun

ames aren't just for social fun. Play is one of the best tools for learning. Enliven your training sessions with activities that help adults to learn even when they think it's just for fun. Some of our favorite resources include the *Games Trainers Play* series, the *Big Book of Business Games,* and *Team Games for Trainers.*

▼   ▼   ▼

"One can discover more about a person in an hour of play than in a year of conversation."

—Plato

▼   ▼   ▼

urprise your newest employees with an orientation they will never forget. To acquaint them with your location, key functions, and important people, create a "scavenger hunt" that requires the new recruits to complete a puzzle that can only be solved by their adventuring around the workplace meeting new

training

coworkers, exploring new departments, and retrieving essential information about different company functions. Learning can be fun, especially when you are not tied to a chair.

You can also create a scavenger hunt of things to find and do in the office. For example, a new hire might be asked to find the copy machine or fax machine or to figure out how to look something up on the computer. The idea is to get the new hire comfortable in their new surroundings and have an informal way for them to meet others in the office. This is also an easy way to train people in standard office procedures and in the use of standard office machines.

Mercer Management Consulting uses this technique to familiarize team members with new cities. MMC has employees find client offices, prominent hotels, and the city's convention center. To prove that they successfully found each "item," they have to bring some proof back to the office, such as client business cards or an exhibitor's name badge.

fun

E ven the driest material can be made fun with games. Joe Mullenax of the Hoechst Celanese Chemical Group encourages trainers to make required training subjects entertaining by using game formats like bingo, Jeopardy, or Concentration. He explains, "The games help employees to not dread training and facilitate discussion and interactions that might not otherwise occur."

▼   ▼   ▼

"Frivolity can unleash ingenuity . . . and impulsive acts of silliness can beget exquisite turns of innovation."
—Mark Leibovich, "San Jose Mercury News,"
August 4, 1996

▼   ▼   ▼

S tacy Yusim, curriculum developer for BOCA International, writes, "One of my coworkers and I had two symposiums to coordinate. It was a lot of work. My colleague helped to turn the process into a fun challenge. We 'reeled in' panelists, made a contest of guessing how much help we would need, and went on a 'shopping spree' to find fun giveaways for participants. It's true, time flies when you are having fun. A huge task heaped on an already full plate turned out to be a fun adventure. Both of our symposiums went well. We were calm throughout and received positive and enthusiastic evaluations from the participants."

▼   ▼   ▼

Take mandated training and make it fun. Mary Vondra, coordinator of educational services at Children's Hospital in Omaha, Nebraska, livened up their federally mandated emergency disaster

training. She organized a mock disaster scheduled for late October. Seizing the Halloween spirit, the trainers adopted a Haunted House of Horrors, challenging employees to spot the "horrors" of unsafe situations. The Haunted House, complete with eerie sounds, attracted 575 employee participants, who all gave it a 95 percent or higher success rating.

▼　　▼　　▼

Sandy Tillotson, a trainer, keeps her students' attention by playing a game with them. At the beginning of class, each student picks a card from a deck and then returns that card to the deck. After each lesson Sandy asks a question. The student who correctly answers the question picks a card from the deck. The more correct answers, the more cards a student accumulates. At the end of the class, all students who have picked their original card get to choose a free gift (usually a computer book or disc). The students love it and participate enthusiastically.

Employees from the Colorado Health Sciences Center in Denver who viewed humorous training films and attended workshops showed a 25 percent decrease in downtime and a 60 percent increase in job satisfaction.

—"HR Focus," February 1993

▼   ▼   ▼

Kathleen Erickson Freeman of Interaction Associates shares her company secrets for keeping employees' energy high. "Our company engages in an annual retreat to recharge our batteries and help us connect with each other. We organize fun into every agenda. Some of our favorite retreat team activities include: making a company quilt, roasting and parodying the outgoing employees, and evening skits and songs. At one retreat, we gave everyone a disposable camera. The fun memories were recorded to remind us that we have a frivolous side in future times of stress."

fun

Mary Vondra was a member of a creation team to develop a training program at Children's Hospital in Omaha, Nebraska, that would help nurses recognize empowerment opportunities in the new "shared governance" process to be implemented at the hospital. She told us that the training program was developed around a theme related to being on a train ride together toward shared governance. The instructors wore train hats and red kerchiefs around their necks.

Participants were given train whistles, which added levity and fun to the training. A song was even written and sung to the tune of "I've Been Working on the Railroad." Participants left the training sessions blowing their train whistles and seeming optimistically reenergized about where shared governance could lead the department.

training

T he general manager at the Qua Buick dealership in Cleveland, Ohio, developed a fun and creative way to teach the skill of questioning to his sales staff. He gave each salesperson ten one-dollar bills. For the remainder of the day, every question had to be answered with a question. Anyone caught answering a question without a question was charged a dollar.

"The activity stimulated much creativity and enthusiasm. It served its purpose in focusing our efforts on listening and asking better questions in order to serve the needs of our clients."

▼　　▼　　▼

A ccording to an article in the February 1996 issue of *Training and Development* magazine, Augusta Technical Institute wanted to create a fun, highly interactive, team-building exercise that would help the participants get to know each other. As a result, they created a colorful, decorative "rainbow mosaic" that drew participants into the program, triggered conversations, and initiated thought-provoking questions.

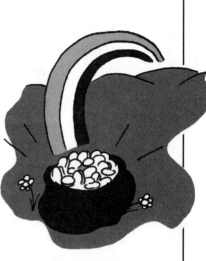

The name "rainbow mosaic" comes from the colorful, mosaic-like wall display that is one result of completing the exercise. In the exercise, participants write on pieces of colored paper their answers to a series of questions that reveal their values and how they view their work relationships. The colored papers are then hung on the walls of a hallway.

Following are some examples of the questions:

▼ What is the most exciting or exotic place you ever visited or vacationed?

▼ What is the most dangerous (exciting, risky, scary) thing you have ever done?

▼ Name a person (celebrity, famous, notorious— living or dead) whom you would like to meet and talk with.

▼   ▼   ▼

Gail Newman of American Management Systems has a career development course for assimilation of new hires just out of college. The training consists of playing "The Game of Life." The object of the game is to successfully navigate your career from graduation through retirement. The game that Gail uses is slightly altered from the Milton Bradley version—the obstacles and career challenges are customized to her specific training issues. Gail feels that using this game for new recruits gives them a nonthreatening, fun way to deal with the important issues of career development.

fun

86

Music is a popular way to generate enthusiasm and interest in many training subjects. Rebecca Rogers, quality improvement facilitator at University Hospitals in Augusta, Georgia, likes to use her "trusty tape" of old TV theme songs to introduce training topics. The theme songs from *Mission Impossible* and *Gilligan's Island* are two training favorites. Rebecca says, "The boomers love it. Generation Xer's look at us like we are dotty old coots, but they know the words too!"

▼   ▼   ▼

George Lindamood of CyberTiger in Sequim, Washington, has found that by adding a little whimsey to his training slides, training becomes much more palatable for everyone. On his slides, George adds a somewhat irreverent quote in small type in a box at the bottom. He call these quotes GUMPS: George's Uninhibited Management Principles.

training

In the nine months that followed a workshop conducted by C. W. Metcalf (humor consultant) at Digital Equipment Corp. in Colorado Springs, twenty middle managers increased their productivity by 15 percent and reduced their sick days by half.

—"HR Focus," February 1993

▼   ▼   ▼

Rhonda Wiley-Jones of Iowa State University in Ames, Iowa, knows the close connection between creativity and learning. For one of her training sessions she came up with a clever new training tool. Rhonda writes: "I asked an artist to design a line drawing of a garden scene that workshop participants could spend the day doodling on and coloring. Four large boulders were included in the picture so that participants could capture the three or four main ideas they want to remember or actions they want to take as a result of the workshop. I supply crayons, colored markers, pencils, and chalk."

fun

This is an inspiring way to use the natural tendencies of workshop participants to doodle, and yet they walk away with the key points of a learning exercise. Their drawings might even look good on the refrigerator.

▼　▼　▼

Olga Rasmussen, a department chair at Georgetown Visitation Preparatory School, tries to mix some true "getting-away" time in with her staff's getting-away time. During a faculty retreat, Olga arranged for everyone to take time out of a very hectic schedule to share the personal talents of colleagues. One woman instructed an audience in how to make a quilt, another taught yoga, and yet another taught poetry writing.

training

"Fun is something that alleviates stress and brings people together, promoting team interactions in a different way than work."

—Trowby Brockman

▼　　▼　　▼

Maria Raper relates her experience at La Quinta Inns: "Each new hire at the corporate office goes to 'Potty School.' They live at one of the inns and work every shift and position, including cleaning the toilets. Upon completion of the school, the employee receives a trophy that has a toilet on it! I proudly display mine even though I don't work there anymore."

▼　　▼　　▼

Along with the overwhelming amount of essential information that is given in a new employee's orientation packet, surprise them with a "humor manual." The manual can be a simple photocopied, bound notebook including cartoons and anecdotes. The Original Copy Center, headquartered in Cleveland, Ohio, used their humor manual as a promotional giveaway at trade shows. Their booth was always swamped with requests for the popular document.

▼   ▼   ▼

As an ice-breaking exercise or as a way to introduce new people to a company, you can create a crossword puzzle or word scramble with everyone's names included.

▼   ▼   ▼

C. W. Metcalf, a leader in humor consulting, has produced a video entitled "Humor, Risk, and Change" that deals with stress in the workplace. It is available from American Media. For more information, call 800-262-2557. C. W. also has published a best-selling book, "Lighten Up." To order it, call 800-968-9622.

training

According to Brenda Paik in the September 1995 issue of the *Personnel Journal,* new hires at Southwest Airlines are required to watch a series of orientation videos. The first video is called *The Southwest Airlines Shuffle.* It incorporates rap music performed by various employees who describe their job duties. Even Herb Kelleher, president of Southwest, appears as Big Daddy-O.

▼　　▼　　▼

"When work is a pleasure, life is a joy! When work is a duty, life is slavery."

—Maxim Gorky

▼　　▼　　▼

Nokia Mobile Phones of San Diego, California, uses the buddy system for employee orientation. New hires are assigned a "buddy" who shows them around the office, takes them to lunch on their first day, and helps them to fully set up their new work space (including mounting a name plate). Nokia also gives new hires welcoming gifts—a T-shirt and a coffee mug to commemorate their first day with the company.

▼　　▼　　▼

While providing computer training, David Bryson, trainer/facilitator for Software Training Service, Inc., reinforces key ideas for learners with barn animal sounds. For example, he has been known to holler "Shewee" to let someone know that they are hogging the computer.

▼　　▼　　▼

"In training classes, fun creates enthusiasm and excitement plus bewilderment. I think people are motivated by the excitement of doing non-traditional activities in the workplace."

—Isabella LaBarbera,
Senior Program Administrator, Com Ed

training

FUN FOCUS

LEARNING IS FUN AT THE STORE OF KNOWLEDGE

How much fun can public television be? A lot—if the Store of Knowledge, a Los Angeles-based toy company, is any indication. The first thing you notice when you walk into the Store of Knowledge is that everyone is playing with something, including the employee at the door whose job it is to interest you in their gadget.

And when you take a look around at the gizmos and gadgets available at the Store of Knowledge, interest is, well, a no-brainer.

A PLAY-FOR-PROFIT ORGANIZATION

The Store of Knowledge is a cooperative effort of Lakeshore Learning Materials and public television. Its goal is to provide life-long learning opportunities to the community, and in the process, to support public television both financially and conceptually. Lakeshore is a $100 million catalog-sales organization that is one of the leading providers of high-quality educational products. Additionally, Lakeshore operates six retail outlets that sell toys, educational products, and teaching supplies.

"Play" is the operative word at the Store of Knowledge, and with play comes fun. Everything here is meant to be

fun

played with. The goal of the employees, who are specially selected for their congeniality and inquisitiveness, is to engage the customer, to get the customer to play with the toys, gizmos, games, and gadgets, because the first rule of selling is to make the customer comfortable with new things and new ideas. And there's no better way to get comfortable than to play with something yourself.

The Los Angeles public television station's KCET Store of Knowledge was the first to open in the spring of 1994. In November of 1996, the Strongsville, Ohio, public television station's WVIZ Store of Knowledge became the twenty-fifth store in the chain. Public television holds an equity share in the Store of Knowledge and shares in the royalties. In fact, each store is legally named for the public television station in its area.

Because of its public television connection, the Store of Knowledge carries a lot of Public Broadcasting Service (PBS) program-related material, from Barney to Pavarotti. In the children's area of each store, television monitors, located conveniently only six inches off the floor, play a seemingly endless schedule of children's programming on public television.

ENTERTAIN YOUR BRAIN

"Public television?" you might say, "I thought that was dull and boring." But the Store of Knowledge is consistently the busiest store in the mall, wherever it may be located. When other stores have three or four customers, the Store of Knowledge can be counted on to have thirty or forty. The WVIZ Store of Knowledge was so busy in its third week of operation, for example, that they had twenty-two people

training

working overnight just to restock the shelves!

The average length of stay per customer at a Store of Knowledge is more than one hour! Any sales manager can tell you, the longer customers stay and the more involved they are with the product, the more likely they are to buy. Fun definitely sells.

The phenomenal success of the Store of Knowledge is due to its philosophy, a philosophy that encourages the customer to have fun by playing with the products before buying them . . . and play, and play, and play.

Isn't it surprising what you can learn from public television?

MEETINGS

HAVING FUN—WISH YOU WERE HERE

HAVING FUN— WISH YOU WERE HERE

American businesspeople spend millions of hours in meetings each year. Are we accomplishing the results to justify this investment of time?

| fun | can be the catalyst for an effective meeting. Used appropriately, fun and humor can relieve meeting tedium and level the hierarchical playing field to create an atmosphere that encourages honest dialogue, risk taking, and the sharing of ideas.

Make the most of your **meetings** by making them more effective. Challenge yourself to incorporate several new ideas into the design of your next meeting. Adults learn and retain information best through interaction and involvement. Individuals process information best when you can stimulate their senses. Take advantage of these special opportunities every time you gather by giving your coworkers something to look at, something to listen to, and something to do.

enliven your meetings and presentations with a sense of humor and fun and find out how productive and creative your **coworkers** can be.

The Liberty Toy Company has found that the best way to get their staff members to talk freely and share ideas is to arm them with foam darts. Typical conference combatants are salespeople and accountants, who are able to take out their frustrations in a harmless fight before sitting down to business. Liberty Toy has realized that a fun icebreaker is sometimes the best start to a productive meeting. They have given their staff many different toys to play with, but by far the most popular are the toy guns and darts.

A lot of fun can be had with popular soft foam toys. By far the best selection of foam toys are made by Kenner, under the brand name Nerf. Our favorites are the Nerf Arrowstorm, the Nerf Sharpshooter, and any of the numerous Nerf footballs. Kenner is a division of Hasbro Toys, headquartered in Pawtucket, Rhode Island, and can be reached at 401-431-8697.

fun

M any successful companies outline the upcoming year's goals and business agenda at a meeting at the beginning of the fiscal year. Why not do what Alltel Corporate Services in Little Rock, Arkansas, does? They put on a skit that highlights all the company issues for the upcoming year, including corporate objectives. The most recent annual meeting featured a skit based on *The Wizard of Oz*. The company then returned to this theme to reenforce goals and objectives throughout the year. They truly followed the yellow brick road!

▼　　▼　　▼

A fter a particularly stressful week of training, Mayo Neyland of the Texas Association of School Boards hosted a staff get together called a "wind down." Mayo and her staff got creative and decided that wind down could also be "whine down" or even "wine down." Regardless of what they called it, the results were fun. What a great way to relieve stress and have fun at the end of a job well done.

"Don't worry, be happy!"

—Bobby McFerrin, musician

▼　　▼　　▼

S tart your meeting by asking everyone to complete an open-ended grabber of a sentence:

"Wouldn't it be fun if . . ." or "The funniest thing I've seen at work is . . ."

Don't be surprised if it takes some time to stimulate the fun juices. Once those juices get going, however, you will have created an energy boost for the remainder of your meeting.

Another meeting starter idea is to write on a flip chart or white board things like

"the word of the day" or a phrase such as "If I were president, I would . . ." or "My greatest pet peeve is . . ."

and ask people to make a list. This is a great warm-up exercise to get people thinking creatively at the beginning of a meeting.

fun

An effective way to teach meeting dynamics is to have meeting participants role-play a mock meeting. Use common meeting personalities—like the interrupter, the babbler, the sleeper, and the master of the obvious. The participants will share in the humor of meeting situations and retain most of information.

DILBERT reprinted by permission of United Feature Syndicate, Inc.

meetings

velyn and Fran Girard, owners of the Forum Conference Center, are always looking for new and different ways to attract organizations to their location for meetings. Recently they unveiled a secret weapon—their Pow! kit. Meeting planners can arrange to have a Pow! kit, containing soft baseball bats, Nerf balls, dart guns, balsa airplanes, and other fun surprises, in the meeting room in order to engage the participants in fun. The Girard's clients have told them the Pow! kit helps to stimulate creativity and maintain a relaxed atmosphere. It creates smiles, laughter, and memorable meetings.

FACTS **According to Dr. William Fry of the Stanford University Medical School, laughter can boost cardiovascular fitness by lowering blood pressure and heart rate. It also reduces pain perception, stimulates blood flow, strengthens the immune system, and reduces levels of hormones that create stress, all of which could have positive effects on a person's creativity and productivity.**

—Bradford Swift, "HRMagazine," March 1994

fun

Berrett-Koehler Publishers in San Francisco has several employees who have taken the option to work full-time from their homes. Monthly staff meetings are the only time that the entire staff gets together. In order to keep everyone informed of important information and the goings-on in the company, they schedule a "show-and-tell" into every meeting. Staff members are encouraged to share successes or news in their own work, but it is a time to share silly and personal experiences too. Often staff members will bring in pictures of their vacation, their children, even their pets.

▼　　▼　　▼

A Seattle-based company had become bogged down by meeting blues—so much so that everyone dreaded their monthly meetings. To make the meetings more fun and inviting, several people organized tournaments, which are played during meeting breaks. Most popular is Boggle, a game where you try to create words out of jumbled letters. The tournaments have proved to be both fun and energizing for the staff.

meetings

An Arthur Andersen office has changed their weekly meetings into half-hour "coffee talks" in their open space. The challenge is to find a creative way to share information in a short amount of time. For example, the production group wanted to let everyone know about changes in roles and responsibilities taking place within their department. They prepared a skit, dressed up, and presented a talk show format with Sally Jessy Raphael as the hostess. It was hilarious. Food is available most of the time, which encourages participation. Everyone looks forward to these weekly meetings!

▼   ▼   ▼

Nobody likes to be locked in a room to complete another annual plan or budget. Consider a change in location to energize your

fun

next meeting. Also, a change in environment might produce a change in your thinking.

Joe Mullenax, organizational development coordinator of the Hoechst Celanese Chemical Group, participated in a meeting that took place poolside. Employees were encouraged to dress casually and enjoy lunch in the sun. He observed that everyone was more relaxed and less stressed. As a result, their first meeting on redesign of the company was a huge success.

Dean Martens of the Charles Machine Works in Perry, Oklahoma, keeps his company meetings lively and fun by hosting them in different locations. His favorite sites are the local historical points of interest, which the locals rarely visit. Dean shares the company motto that "It's O.K. to have fun!"

To add fun to your meetings, you may want to consider watching a video called "Meetings Bloody Meetings." This video is produced by Video Arts and stars John Cleese of Monty Python fame. This will certainly add a little British humor to your next meeting.

▼   ▼   ▼

Grace Noonan-Kaye has carried a fun practice over to her current position with the Portland Newspapers. To kick off every staff meeting, people are invited to share their "celebrations," either personal or professional. Everyone is also invited to vent one complaint. This is an excellent way to clear the air before sitting down to business.

fun

Fun is a great way to start a relationship. It can differentiate you from the crowd. If your company uses trade shows as a strategy for client relations, consider incorporating fun and humor into your display.

Ehmke Movers from Cincinnati, Ohio, had the busiest booth at a recent trade show. The participants were all engaged in completing a foam puzzle that was emblazoned with the company logo. The puzzle, called a SnaFooz, has six colorful foam pieces that form a cube (if you're talented enough to figure it out).

While individuals challenged themselves to find the puzzle solution, they were also building relationships with the company representatives staffing the booth. Work and fun can combine to start lasting relationships.

"Fun doesn't stifle, it encourages depth and breadth among work relationships."
—Lee McGrath, Cambria Consulting, Inc.

meetings

The Madison Area Quality Improvement Network in Wisconsin has weekly staff meetings and all staff members take a turn as facilitator. One staff member, acting as facilitator, asked everyone to bring in a baby picture of themselves. Everyone then tried to guess whose baby picture was whose. It proved to be a fun icebreaker for the start of the meeting.

▼   ▼   ▼

Mark Leibovich, in his article "All Work and Some Play" in the August 4, 1996, *San Jose Mercury News*, reports that "Bob Lord, president of Emerge Consulting in Palo Alto [California], attributes some of his company's success to Silly Putty. Employees of his Internet consulting group bring fist-sized gobs into meetings. 'We are idea-based people and Silly Putty makes the ideas come a little more freely,' says Vice President Jeff Leane."

fun

They buy the pliable dough from Sarah Ferguson, a technical staffer known as the Duchess of Chaos. In addition to Silly Putty's signature flesh color, Ferguson pushes pink, yellow, and blue glow-in-the-dark varieties.

▼　　▼　　▼

According to Evelyn Girard of the Forum Conference Center, the most important resource that she has to offer to clients coming to her facility for a meeting is a toy box. She thinks that every conference room should have one—with toys inside to spur creativity, reduce stress, and build teamwork.

▼　　▼　　▼

Human Dynamics, Inc., holds rubber brick meetings: Meeting attendees are encouraged to hurl a rubber brick at coworkers who show up late or say something inappropriate. Most people now show up on time so they can have the opportunity to take out their aggressions on tardy coworkers.

▼   ▼   ▼

M ission statements can sometimes be the most tedious and stuffy prose on earth. One team at University Hospitals in Augusta, Georgia, decided to put their mission statement to a rhyming scheme, which they recite at the beginning of each meeting. When silliness gets the best of them, they have even attempted to recite the mission statement while dancing to the Macarena.

▼   ▼   ▼

M urder mysteries are very popular party games. At a murder mystery party, a group of people act out characters in a predetermined mystery. The characters are slowly given more information about themselves throughout the course of the game until the mystery is solved at the end of the party. One company, Human Dynamics, has added a little fun to their weekly meeting routine by taking a half hour at the beginning of each meeting to play a murder mystery game. Eileen Douse says that this has been an incredible way to more open and creative staff meetings. Interestingly, throughout the entire game, which might last from six to eight weeks, you are never sure whether your coworkers are "in character" or not. Remember: always watch your back!

"The first time I ever participated in a skit as a manager during a company meeting, I realized the power of acting silly, or real, in front of a group. The response, the attitude, even the ultimate respect was overwhelming."

—Cynthia House, quoted in "At Work,"
November/December 1996

meetings

John Case, in his article "Corporate Culture" in the November 1996 issue of *Inc.* magazine, tells about Richard Block, CEO of AGI, Inc., a company in Melrose Park, Illinois, who challenges himself to answer his employees' toughest questions at the company's monthly meetings. In the "Stump-the-CEO Contest," Block allows himself to be interrogated about anything to do with the company. The toughest questioner is rewarded with a prize.

Block feels these sessions help breed an environment of open communication and send the message that they are all accountable to each other. He feels that they "maintain their creative edge by promoting open debate and the

fun

combustive rub of ideas—an environment that is for experimentation and that urges you to take responsibility for a problem instead of working at concealing it."

▼ ▼ ▼

Bradley Wilkinson of Atlanta, Georgia, has successfully moved the kitchen into the meeting room. One of his most productive meetings is the potluck dinner meeting, where attendees each bring a dish to feast upon during the meeting—a more fun and less expensive alternative to a typical restaurant meeting. Another favorite is the "Popcorn Video Preview" meeting, used to preview training films. If you have to sit through a series of training videos, at least be armed with Orville Redenbacher's best.

▼ ▼ ▼

"Fun leads to creativity . . . a spirit of non-judgement where new ideas emerge."
—Dave Whitleng, OOED

meetings

"All work is empty save when there is love."

—Kahlil Gibran

H ealthEast, a health-care concern in St. Paul, Minnesota, uses food in a slightly bizarre way. Carolyne Check describes a common meeting: "One group meets weekly to plan strategy for the organization. A totally petrified banana is brought to each meeting and passed around as an "award" for different activities. The banana was originally found in an old desk drawer in the meeting room and is now a mascot and science experiment all in one. This has been going on for nearly two years. It sounds ridiculous, but we enjoy it."

▼   ▼   ▼

S ometimes our focus at a meeting is directed toward what's not working instead of the urgent problems that need to be addressed.

fun

Reenergize your meeting by acknowledging someone who has done something that exemplifies the mission of the organization. Recognize that individual with a standing ovation.

▼　　▼　　▼

Many companies are using a derivation from Edward DeBono's book *Six Thinking Hats*. The basic idea is that during a meeting participants figuratively or in reality don different colored hats to represent different ways of thinking. For example, the person wearing the blue hat would be responsible for looking at things from the big picture perspective (or blue sky), the person wearing the black hat would be the devil's advocate, and the person wearing the green hat would be the optimist. You can pick your own colors and meanings or use DeBono's book. Either way, this is a great tool for allowing

MEETING ←

meetings

117

people in a meeting to safely look at issues from different perspectives. Make sure that everyone gets a chance to wear a different colored hat at each meeting.

▼ ▼ ▼

DAVE'S (HEMSATH)
TOP TEN LIST

of most admired fun companies (as compiled from our surveys):

10. Motorola

9. Arthur Andersen

8. Walmart

7. Nordstrom

6. EDS

5. Hewlett Packard

4. Microsoft

3. Ben and Jerry's

2. Southwest Airlines, and

#1. Disney

fun

ccording to Paul Phillips, GTE Data Services in Fort Wayne, Indiana, has established a fun meeting tradition—the facilitator of their weekly meetings wears a Goofy (the Disney character) hat during the meeting. The facilitator changes for each meeting, so everyone gets a chance to act goofy. During the meeting, participants are on the lookout for the "Funny Quote of the Meeting," a funny misstatement that is published in the meeting minutes.

▼   ▼   ▼

urina Bakken of MAQIN in Madison, Wisconsin, holds staff meetings twice per month and has been able to bring a lot of fun to these meetings. Following are some examples:

▼ The staff went out into the parking lot with three beach balls. We started with one ball and had to keep it up in the air. Then we added a second ball and the third into the circle. It got pretty crazy. Then we threw in a ball with sand in it, so it bounced funny. When we came back in, we talked about the parallels between trying to keep all those balls up in the air and our work. (Note: Leslie has participated in similar discussions based on teaching people how to juggle.)

▼ We collected baby pictures of all staff and created a who's who game. The winner got a certificate at a malt shop.

▼ When a new staff member joined our meetings, the facilitator wanted to "toast" the new person, so she brought in champagne glasses, juice, and a toaster with bread and a variety of jams. We toasted the new person literally and figuratively!

▼ To help stir our creativity for some new initiatives, one staff member brought in fortune cookies with homemade fortunes baked into them. Each fortune was a question that the whole staff addressed. It really got us thinking out of the box.

fun

According to *Inc.* magazine (November 1996), "Visual In-Seitz, in Rochester, New York, creates business presentations for companies such as Xerox and Kodak. 'Timelines are very short and client demands very high,' says CEO Charles Engler, 'which equals stress.' How to vent it? Hold Thursday afternoon production meetings off-site—at a bar. Employees share problems and tips, track performance, and voice complaints that clients will never hear. The message: we see the pressure you're under, and we value how you handle it."

At least on Thursdays, this is a bar where everyone will know your name.

▼   ▼   ▼

Have fun with your new hires. Consider beginning your next meeting or conference with a "rookie camp" for the newest players on your team. Spend some extra time giving them a "leg up" on the information and expectations of the meeting. Arm them with special name tags to identify them to more tenured employees, who can mentor them through the process. Even consider giving them squirt guns and the instruction to use their water persuasion if the meeting becomes too boring or not meaningful.

D o your meetings dissolve into chaotic free-for-alls? Do coworkers continuously hold sidebar conversations, complete other work, or interrupt one another incessantly? Perhaps you can achieve order through the development of group ground rules. Then provide squirt guns to all  meeting participants, encouraging them to use gentle persuasion on those who stretch the established ground rules. If this doesn't do the trick, pass out blindfolds and attempt to run your meeting sightless. The change of dynamics may help to bring your meeting back into focus.

FUN FOCUS

MEETING MAGIC AND THE FORUM CONFERENCE CENTER

The scene was reminiscent of vaudeville. The delivery man, regular and well known, was giving Fran and Evelyn Girard, owners and managers of the Forum Conference Center in Cleveland, Ohio, a good-natured ribbing about something that was not quite right. Fran said, "Oh yeah?" while Evelyn picked up a squirt bottle filled with water from its home on the corner of Fran's desk and sprayed the delivery man!

What happened next? They all broke into guffaws and the problem was resolved. In addition, everyone got a chuckle out of it all day long, including people who weren't even there!

ALWAYS ROOM FOR FUN

While not exactly an everyday occurrence, this scene typifies the attitude that Fran and Evelyn Girard bring to their work. "In 1990, we started a business that had no frame of reference. We were renting rooms for meetings and conferences without renting the hotel rooms to go with them," recalled Evelyn. "In order to survive, we needed to not only provide top-quality customer service, but also be distinctive."

What makes the Forum distinctive is its superior

meetings

customer service, including attention to detail, a can-do attitude, a professional demeanor, and a great sense of humor. As a result, more than forty thousand people attend meetings at the Forum every year now, and Evelyn greets each one of them personally at the top of the escalator.

Evelyn, Fran, and their twenty employees have fun at work, and they try to see to it that their guests have fun too! "One of these days I'm going to get punched out," Fran says, with more than a touch of glee. Fran has been known to respond to the question "Where are your rest rooms?" with the unexpected reply, "We don't have any." Fortunately, this sort of off-the-wall response usually draws a deep, rolling chuckle from the guest: after the initial shock wears off!

"If you can't go to work and have fun," Fran adds, "then it's not worth going." Evelyn makes her own contribution to the merriment by answering questions like, "How do I get to the Forum from Solon?" with "You can't get here from there!"

BIG-HITTING FUN

Lest you think Fran and Evelyn are all yuks and backslaps, you need to know about their marketing savvy, which, as you might expect, includes humor. Marketing 101 says the best way to improve your bottom line is to get your current customers to buy more. The Girards have done just that, while at the same time injecting their sense of fun into their POW! kit.

The POW! kit is something different and unexpected. Fran explains, "We offer the kit to our clients for their meetings. A POW! kit is a package of toys, like Nerf footballs, basketball hoops and Nerf balls, Zoomballs, Styrofoam darts, or golf stress relievers. These items help the attendees to interact with each other, think more

fun

creatively, and be more relaxed."

"It makes them smile," Evelyn adds, "which leads to laughter and makes brainstorming and creative thinking all the more effective. And when their meetings are over, everyone agrees on how productive they were, how much they learned, and how much fun they had, so we get tons of repeat bookings. During annual meeting time, it can be hard to find an open room to hold a meeting."

MEETING UP WITH FUN

One day, a few minutes after the annual meeting for a very large and successful bank began, an elderly gentleman came up the escalator and was greeted by Fran, who walked with him toward the meeting room. "You must own a lot of stock," the man said to Fran, "I see you here every year!"

"Once you open the door to fun," Evelyn says, "you invite people to engage you on another level. The fun we have with our guests creates relationships—and that's good for both the Forum and the company renting our space, not to mention Fran and me and the whole staff."

"The Forum Conference Center proves," Fran says, "that you can be professional and have fun at the same time; they are not incompatible. In fact, they really go hand in hand. We take our business and our fun seriously. And that's no joke."

meetings

RECOGNITION

SAY IT WITH FUN

RECOGNITION

SAY IT WITH FUN

Recognition is one of the most powerful and underutilized management tools. Everyone wants recognition. Everyone needs it. And recognition increases the likelihood that the action recognized will be repeated. So why don't we lavish each other with this vital tonic?

We know that when efforts to recognize individuals are mixed with a flavor of fun, they tend to take on a life of their own, creating a more memorable experience. And isn't that the objective in recognizing someone?

It helps to remember that adults are just grown-up kids. We don't grow out of our need for **acknowledgment**, acceptance, fun, and play. We fool ourselves into thinking that to be an adult means to be serious when all it really means is to have aged.

When we let loose the big kid in each of us, we unleash a source of power, energy, and enthusiasm that turns challenges into achievements. Reinforce these achievements **with** zany, memorable acts of recognition and you have a winning combination—a workplace that motivates, empowers, and is downright **fun**.

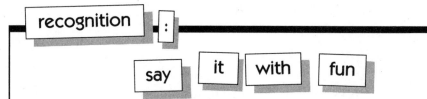

say it with fun

Behavioralists know that if you want to reinforce a habit just recognize that habit. To extinguish a habit ignore or apply a consequence to the habit. Simply psychology. So if you want to improve attendance, reward good attendance.

Consider a fun twist to your recognition effort. Scott Friedman of Denver, Colorado, encourages companies to allow individuals the opportunity to take "well days." Provide employees with "well-day" cards that they can turn in just like you would a "get-out-of-jail-free" card in a monopoly game.

▼ ▼ ▼

Have a department bake sale. At a San Francisco-based publisher, one department had a traditional Friday morning bake sale. By the end of the year, they had raised enough money for a departmental celebration of company and individual successes.

fun

"A light-hearted event can dissolve the daily tension."
—Tom Ziska, Jr., Ziska Architects and Associates

▼　　▼　　▼

A common problem in many offices is recognizing the efforts of individuals who cover for vacationing coworkers. The Donaghey Student Center at the University of Arkansas in Little Rock creates a new award to give to those who do the covering.

For example, "The (choose the name of the appropriate vacationing employee) Award is given to (name of the appropriate vacation slave), who went above and beyond the call of duty to see that the entire infrastructure of this office environment did not collapse in the absence of (vacationing employee). We recognize and appreciate his/her contributions to the successful and smooth operation of this office."

recognition

131

n the process of designing and building an office environment that would facilitate the work of our organization well and embody the spirit of our mission and values, I learned about the power and influence of recognition and fun.

As I supervised the construction space, I adopted a fun ritual. Each day when the different workmen completed their projects, I joyfully inspected their work, excited about the progress toward a visionary design. One day, on impulse, I did a jig as an enthusiastic gesture of my pleasure in their work. The next day I invited one of the tradesmen to join me in my dance. Soon it became an expectation that when work was completed we would engage in a ritual dance, not unlike the end-zone dance performed by football players, to celebrate a step toward the completion of our new offices. Each dance was unique to the individual.

One day, nearing the completion of the project, two older electricians came to finalize some special lighting. They looked at me with

fun

132

some hesitation and quietly asked, "Are you going to make us dance?" I was surprised that word of our festive ritual had spread throughout the trades. I responded just as quietly saying, "Only if you want to." When they had completed their task they sought me out and asked me to look at their work. I bubbled with enthusiasm for a job well done and explained the importance of their special lights.

Wanting to display sensitivity in valuing differences, I did not impose my dance upon these two seasoned electricians. They, however, stood quietly, not ready to leave the space, and volunteered, "Well, are we gonna dance?" I discovered that everyone, regardless of their initial resistance, wants to have fun and relishes the recognition. With tool belts jingling, we danced together.

recognition

U se fun and humorous gifts as recognition items. Some of our favorites are Robert Fulghum's books, starting with *All I Really Need to Know I Learned in Kindergarten,* the *Chicken Soup for the Soul* series by Jack Canfield and Mark Victor Hansen, anything by Og Mandino, and the *Life's Little Instruction Book* series.

An irreverent supplier of fun accessories is Archie McPhee & Co., "Outfitters of Popular Culture." Their catalog is forty-five pages of fun, weird, and disgusting things to add to anyone's fun survival kit. Popular items include propeller beanies, a wide variety of fake eyeballs, rubber chickens, and pink flamingos. To order a catalog, call 206-745-0711 or email them at mcphee@mcphee.com.

fun

Each year Manco, a manufacturer of duct tape, hosts the Annual Duck Challenge to recognize the achievement of company goals. The ritual started when company president Jack Kahl challenged the sales team to meet an aggressive sales goal. He struck an agreement with the sales team: If they met their goal, he would swim across the pond located in front of the company headquarters; if they didn't meet their goal, they would don their bathing suits for a dip.

Sound easy? Not so. The swim would occur during the chilly days of October in northeastern Ohio.

The sales team enthusiastically accepted the challenge and achieved their goal. Jack did ceremoniously swim the length of the pond bedecked in his favorite Speedo swim suit.

This event generated so much interest within and outside of the company that it has become an annual event. Many associates and company partners join in the festivities of a fall dip followed by a company picnic and awards ceremony to celebrate the well-being of this growing enterprise.

recognition

Everybody loves to celebrate a birthday. Double the celebrations by recognizing the anniversary of each employee's hiring date. Make the most of the opportunity to take a quick energy break to rally the troops in acknowledging the contribution of the featured employee.

Here are the ten best ways to reward good work:

1. Money

2. Recognition

3. Time off

4. A piece of the action

5. Favorite work

6. Advancement

7. Freedom

8. Personal growth opportunities

9. "Fun"

10. Prizes

—Michael LeBoeuf, 'The Greatest Management Principle in the World,' in "People Performance" magazine, October 1996

fun

According to *HRMagazine* (March 1994), Wells Fargo Bank in California started a peer reward and recognition program with a twist. The bank awarded $35 gift certificates to all employees. The twist was that the employees couldn't cash in their own certificates; they had to give their certificate to another employee who they believed had done the best job in supporting them.

Those people were then given a banquet hosted by the chairman of the board and the president. During the banquet they had the opportunity to select an award from a list of over one hundred items. Some of the choices were:

▼ A day on a Wells Fargo television commercial shoot
▼ The "shotgun" position on the Wells Fargo stagecoach in a local parade
▼ A visit to their child's school or club meeting by a senior executive

recognition

> **"Creating a fun workplace environment requires a positive view of humanity that begins with the people who work in the corporation."**
>
> **—Dennis Bakke, President, AES Corp.**

▼ ▼ ▼

At Arthur Andersen, one woman celebrated her fifteen-year anniversary with the firm and was treated as "Queen for a Day." The director met her in the parking lot and helped carry her briefcase in as her coworkers rolled out the red carpet and treated her to a corporate massage.

▼ ▼ ▼

Paychecks are generally used to reward employees. Paychecks can also be used to send fun messages or to recognize top performers and employee anniversaries. You can also use paycheck stubs to send messages that recognize

fun

attendance or number of days without an accident, or to send holiday greetings. Be creative. You can be sure that this is one companywide message that everyone will read.

Rewarding employees with an evening out on the town may not be the most prudent thing to do from a liability standpoint. I have found that supplying a driver, or even a limousine, makes for a safe and more memorable night on the town for an employee or work team.

A favorite way to recognize employees and celebrate the successes of a business is to create a "wall of fame." Anything that can personalize the wall, such as photographs of work associates, a map indicating everyone's hometown, even drawings and achievements from coworkers' children, is a special way to recognize each person as an individual.

Following are the top motivating techniques as reported by employees:
   1. Personal thanks
   2. Written thanks
   3. Promotion for performance
   4. Public praise
   5. Morale-building meetings
    —Dr. Gerald Graham, Wichita State University,
   "People Performance" magazine, October 1996

Southwest Airlines is so proud of its star employees that it lets the whole world know. Each year their most recognized employees win the Heroes of the Heart Award. The winners' names appear on a banner painted across a red heart on the nose of an airplane for one year.

▼   ▼   ▼

A West Coast restaurant wanted to create a graphic design for an upcoming advertising campaign. Instead of hiring a professional artist, they encouraged their own employees to submit drawings. What made this really fun was that all the entries had to be submitted using crayons and the "butcher paper" that they use as table covers. The entire staff had a wonderful time creating a drawing that best symbolized the atmosphere of the restaurant. The winning entry was not only used for advertising but also proudly framed and displayed in the restaurant for all to see.

recognition

L aura Simonds of Davies Black Publishing shares a story of a previous employer's tradition that left a memorable impression on her. The organization held an annual celebration called the "Sweet and Sour Awards." The celebration was entirely humorous and meant to be fun. It was organized like the Academy Awards. Prizes were given to the best in categories, such as the best group of babes and hunks, most difficult client, best excuse for a production delay, etc. The prizes were either sweet (like ice cream and cookies) or sour (like pickles). Anyone in the organization could submit a category and suggest a winner. It was a fun event and full of big belly laughs. They were careful not to intentionally hurt anyone and to include everyone.

▼   ▼   ▼

T here isn't a person I know who doesn't like a surprise delivery. My favorite way to brighten the day of an employee, colleague, or client is to send a bouquet of balloons. A big

fun

142

bunch of colorful balloons being carried through the office and arriving unexpectedly at someone's desk can create real excitement. Take the fun a little bit further by visualizing this floating "party in the making" delivered by an individual dressed in a pink gorilla suit. What a fun way to recognize a relationship.

At an EDS office in Plano, Texas, coworkers are recognized for their achievements, anniversaries, or birthdays. According to Anne Liptak of EDS, instead of making it a day for any given individual, outings are planned for the entire team. It might be lunch together or a movie. The key is to celebrate success with all the coworkers who make that success possible. This is a great way to encourage team members to look for ways to acknowledge the efforts of their coworkers.

recognition

At a small but growing Internet marketing company in North Carolina, the president recognized that the staff was starting to feel the pressures that many emerging companies experience. During one pay period he included a certificate for a free massage at a local health spa. The letter recognized the "heavy lifting" the team had been doing, trying to get the company off the ground.

▼   ▼   ▼

FACTS **In a survey of 329 company executives, 97 percent agreed that humor is valuable in business and 60 percent felt that a sense of humor can be a deciding factor in determining how successful a person can be in the business world. In another survey, conducted by Burke Marketing Research, 84 percent of the personnel directors interviewed said that employees with a sense of humor do better work.**

—Terry Braverman, "Training and Development" magazine, July 1993

fun

The Academy Awards ceremony each year recognizes and honors the achievements of individuals in the motion picture industry. Workers at Northlake College in Irving, Texas, also get the opportunity to acknowledge and recognize the achievements of their coworkers each year. Categories are selected, staffers are nominated, and awards are presented at a mock Academy Awards celebration dinner. What a wonderful way to play with a ceremony that has become a part of our culture. Nothing could be as thrilling as hearing your name called out after "and the winner is . . ."

▼　　▼　　▼

At SciQuest in Research Triangle Park, North Carolina, every employee gets their birthday off as a paid holiday. Like any other holiday, if a particular birthday falls on a weekend or other holiday, the next workday can be taken off in celebration.

recognition

"Fun helps to create a comfortable, creative atmosphere where communication is free flowing and employees are energized and enjoy striving for excellence."

—Jim Paluch, J.P. Horizons Inc.

▼ ▼ ▼

Instead of giving plaques or certificates for jobs well done, the fun people at Optimal-Care, Inc., like to give humorous awards that relate specifically to the achievement being recognized. For example, one employee once received a very large spider with "5,000" painted on its back to represent that she recorded the 5,000th "bug" or enhancement suggestion for the particular product.

▼ ▼ ▼

In an attempt to bring people together, one Arizona company created the "Fat-Free Pretzel Barrel" as a gathering place for fun and snacks.

fun

The popular, old television program *This Is Your Life* creates a fun format for recognition. Combine childhood photos, early employment experiences, and coworkers' stories to entertain everyone and recognize an individual for their contributions.

▼   ▼   ▼

"Fun is when you really enjoy what you are doing and the people you are doing it with, and much is being accomplished."
—Phyllis Van, Organizational Effectiveness Specialist, Rockwell-Collins Businesses

▼   ▼   ▼

Maria Raper, who works for the city of Austin, Texas, uses food to properly recognize her coworkers. When congratulating someone for a job well done, Maria passes out "Kudos" candy bars; she gives out "Lifesavers" to those whose efforts have been real lifesavers.

recognition

reate mini theme parties. For example, one company in Minnesota celebrates large and small successes by hosting "high tea" instead of the typical coffee break. Everyone brings a tea cup and wears a hat to set the tone.

Most office activities, no matter how small, could be turned into mini theme parties with a little creativity. Office personnel could wear brown outfits to recognize the UPS delivery person or get together for a break with sunglasses or mittens for Ground Hog day. I am sure you can come up with inventive ways to spend ten minutes recognizing one another or celebrating a success.

For those of you who would like to host office theme parties but are having trouble coming up with original ideas, a book by Ellen Hoffman called "Rock the Casbah: The Complete Guide to Hosting Your Own Theme Party" might help. The cost is $12.95 and it should be available in most bookstores.

C apital One Services in Tampa, Florida, recognizes employees' birthdays and anniversaries by building a Styrofoam cake and placing it above the person's cubicle during the month of the celebration. (I hope no one is required to eat the cake at the end of the month.)

Another Capital One activity is that employees give their peers raffle tickets in recognition of a job well done. The tickets can be redeemed at month-end raffle drawings. This is a great tool for encouraging coworkers to be conscious of each other's contributions.

recognition

Paul Phillips, manager of Production Support for GTE Data Services, describes how his company recognizes effort: "One of our most popular ways to recognize the entire group (about eighty people) is to have a 'movie afternoon.' We arrange with a local theater to run a tab for us for the tickets and at the concession stand. Employees show up with a letter from us for admission, get some popcorn, candy, or whatever they want, and spend an afternoon playing hooky from work while enjoying a movie with coworkers at the company's expense. This is an inexpensive way to recognize people (about ten dollars per person), and it makes a lasting impression on the employees. Those who can't attend because of work commitments are given two movie passes to use at their convenience."

▼   ▼   ▼

"It has been my experience that fun arises naturally out of the mixture of the right people and satisfying work."
—Barry Jonahsen, College Hill Group

fun

DAVE'S (HEMSATH)

TOP TEN LIST

of most popular fun recognition gifts (as compiled from our surveys):

10. **Gag gifts**
9. **Popcorn tins or fruit baskets**
8. **Plaques and trophies**
7. **Books (Dave's favorite idea)**
6. **Tickets to a sports event**
5. **Balloons (with or without the gorilla delivery)**
4. **Gift certificates (to almost anything)**
3. **Dinner out (lunch and breakfast as well)**
2. **T-Shirts, and**
#1. **Coffee mugs (preferably with a cartoon)**

▼   ▼   ▼

G raduates from the Leadership Academy at HealthEast in St. Paul, Minnesota, are asked to come up with creative presentations for

recognition

a cocktail party that is held to celebrate their course completion. The graduates typically come up with poems or rap songs based on what they have learned and perform them at the party.

▼ ▼ ▼

D onald Willens, affectionately known as the King of Cartoons, wears a crown while sitting at his desk at Animation, U.S.A., in San Francisco. Donald exudes enthusiasm for his job and professes he has fun every day. His coworkers presented him with a crown as a tribute to his unbridled passion for his work. He says all his childhood television watching has paid off big. He has translated his love for cartoon characters into a career. His enthusiasm is contagious and fosters immediate client relations and sales. Like the character animations he promotes, every "cel" of his person screams "have fun." It's all about taking the fun of your life and bringing it into your work.

fun

FUN FOCUS

HIGH-FLYING FUN AT MANCO

Manco is a privately owned corporation headquartered in Avon, Ohio, that specializes in the manufacture of tape, packaging, and weather-stripping products. From the physical layout of their new offices to their ever-present mascot, Manco T. Duck, company leader Jack Kahl has worked to create an atmosphere that encourages employees (called partners in Manco lingo) to be creative, to communicate well with one another, and to aggressively look for opportunities to have fun. Manco's formula for success is a culture based on trust and empowerment. The company is regularly recognized not only as a leader in their industry but also as a leader in business management.

TOP-FLIGHT DUCKS

Manco's products are sold in a variety of retail and wholesale outlets throughout the United States, including office supply stores, hardware stores, home centers, and discount chains; their products are also sold in fifty-nine other countries via direct Manco accounts, hardware co-ops, and military px programs. Manco has grown from annual sales of $800,000 in 1971 to over $145 million by 1996.

Duck Tape is Manco's most widely recognized product, and mascot Manco T. Duck is the company spokesperson. Today, Duck Tape is number one in

recognition

total sales, owning an impressive 63.3 percent share of the duct tape market. Manco is also the market leader in masking tape, carpet tape, electrical tape, and carton-sealing tape.

Manco is well known for its cultural values of caring and community involvement. Their new headquarters, a 387,000-square-foot facility located on over two hundred acres of land in a small community twenty miles west of Cleveland, reflects a true partnership between Manco, local civic leaders, and the community. The facility is located on Just Imagine Drive, a street named after the corporate slogan, "Just Imagine what our Duck can do for You!" Manco committed up to $100,000 for road improvements and sewer and water assessments on behalf of their new neighbors. Approximately 35 percent of Manco's total property has been set aside as protected wetlands. The local schools also benefit from generous donations to their general fund.

LIFE ON THE DUCK POND

At Manco, fun and creativity thrive in an environment that insists on open communication, freedom of information, and most importantly trust. Manco feels that trust is the keystone to everything that the corporation values. Trust builds a sense of community both within and outside of the organization, and allows partners (employees), customers, and suppliers to invest emotionally in the success of Manco. This investment and trust gives Manco partners the confidence to take risks, enjoy the work process, and have fun. The result is a remarkable company spirit, loyalty, and teamwork. This strategy has not only been successful in creating an effective work environment but has also been key

fun

in building the business.

The free flow of information begins in an intensive training program at Manco University. The training is conducted over three days by twenty-seven different people representing many of the departments throughout the company. The focus is on company values, culture, and history. Communication is maintained by company meetings held twice a week. These meetings are unusual in that they are open to all employees and there is no agenda. They are modeled on a town-meeting format. The primary purpose is to share information, for example, a new idea, competitive news, a success story, a departmental concern, or even a joke. (They have a bell to gong bad jokes.) Unlike many corporations, Manco partners gain influence and stature by building a reputation for sharing information.

GONE QUACKERS

Fun is a result of Manco's core values and vision, but Manco is also known for some rather unusual behavior from their partners. During their annual Duck Challenge Day, Manco partners are at their most creative. This talent contest features many wacky singing, dancing, and other creative presentations.

The Just Imagine Duck Challenge is an opportunity to create and market new products built from Manco products. Entries this year included "Flip Floobes" (flip-flops made out of tape and packaging tubes), a person-alized robot, pot holders, even a football stadium. Everyone gets to vote on the craziest entry.

Manco is particularly known for swimming in the duck pond in recognition of their top sales performers. (See the Manco story on page 135.)

recognition

The corporate offices have street signs labeling each hallway and corridor: Innovation Alley, Quackers Boulevard, Teamwork Way, and University Boulevard take you throughout this dynamic office.

"Trust allows us to have fun," says Kevin Krueger, director of communication and education. "Our customers, our suppliers, and our partners enjoy working with us, which in the end helps to build our business."

TEAM BUILDING

HOW TO CREATE
FUN-ATICS

HOW TO CREATE FUN-ATICS

fun is a social glue: it fosters relationships between individuals in teams; it develops the trust necessary for high-performance teamwork; it soothes the natural tensions that arise when people work together; it is fundamental to teams experiencing the satisfaction of creating something larger than themselves.

Fun **and** productivity are not mutually exclusive.

Bob Filipczak, staff editor of *Training* magazine, retells a story related to him by Matt Weinstein, a humor consultant and founder of the company Playfair, Inc., about an employee who proved to his boss that his team could both "have their cake and eat it too" in combining work with fun.

This is the story of an employee who approached his manager with a fun idea. The worker suggested that on the first day of spring employees be allowed to go outside and stage a paper airplane flying contest. The manager didn't see any point in this nonsense and called the idea insane. The intrepid employee, after talking with his coworkers, made a counterproposal: If the team met 150 percent of its production goal by 3 p.m. Friday, would the manager give the members one hour off for their contest? Sure enough, they met the quota and the manager let them go out and play . Afterward the manager said, "If you could produce this well with an hour off, think of how much you could get done if you worked the whole day" (totally missing the point).

The next week, the employees proposed the same deal—but this time if the workers made the quota, the manager would have to take them all out for ice cream. At this point, says Weinstein, the manager finally got the message: Fun and productivity are not mutually exclusive but are in fact complementary.

Build some zaniness into your team and find out how much more productive and fun working with your teammates can be.

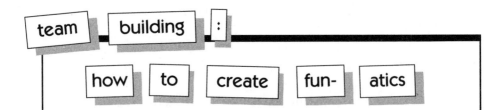

how **to** **create** **fun-** **atics**

he August 1995 issue of *Agency Sales* magazine suggests encouraging employees to take a humor break once a day. A group humor break can help to build teams, improve communication within the group, and increase employee morale. The traditional morning coffee break can be transformed easily into a morning humor break. Humorous pictures and quotes posted in the office break room can facilitate the flow of fun and humor.

ccording to Teresa Perry of Informix Software in Menlo Park, California, one of the company's sales teams brewed beer as a group project. After they formed their team, they went to San Francisco's Brew City, a personal brewery, to mix the wort, ferment the brew, and bottle the beer. By the time their sales project was complete, the beer had aged properly and they were able to celebrate the successful end of their project with the fruit (or hops) of their own labor.

fun

To help foster teamwork within my company, a couple of times throughout the year our entire office will go to a Cleveland Indians baseball game. We start with a tailgate party in the office parking lot and then spend the rest of the day or evening at the ballpark. I have found that turning our offices from a place of work into a party place can have a lasting effect on the staff. Not only do I get to smell stale beer and cigarette smoke for several days afterward, we gain the camaraderie of a shared fun experience. It is hard to get too upset with a coworker you were just "high-fiving" the night before.

A common summer practice in many offices is the company golf outing. Although a golf outing may be fun it unfortunately excludes anyone who doesn't play golf. An EDS office found a way to revise the golf outing to include everyone. In the office, each department created a miniature-golf hole through their own department. They used whatever they could find—binders, desks, chairs—to create obstacles for the "golfers." Each department offered refreshments and custom-decorated their "hole." The result was a company function that built a sense of departmental pride.

I f employees fear making mistakes, they will stop taking risks. To create an environment where mistakes are seen as opportunities to learn, Steve Wilson suggests creating an "UH-OH Squad." To be a member of the "UH-OH Squad" you must follow these simple instructions:

1. Recruit and designate UH-OH Squad members at home, in your office, department, classroom, or wherever.
2. Issue each UH-OH Squad member their official equipment (a red clown nose).
3. Train each squad member thoroughly.
4. Instruct coworkers, family members, or any other group members that in the event of any

fun

stress, frustration, aggravation, annoyance, glitch, or just for fun, they may sound the UH-OH Alert: "I need the UH-OH Squad!!!"

5. Squad members will promptly assemble around the problem, put on their equipment, and stand around chanting, "UH-OH! UH-OH! UH-OH!." An UH-OH Alert should last no more than about one minute, then, back to work.

To receive Steve Wilson's original "UH-OH Squad" equipment, call 800-NOW-LAFF.

A t a San Francisco-based publisher, the office staff often tries to organize informal outings to movies, virtual reality stores, local breweries, and so on. To help facilitate this, they put up a white board in the lunch room so that anyone can post ideas of things to do together. Staff members who are interested can list their

teams

names and help organize the outing together. The "social board" is constantly full of fun and exciting ideas.

At the Arthur Andersen Center for Professional Education, a work team created several fun activities to help people use their imaginations. Recently they have used the letters in a team member's name to explore words and phrases that can be made out of those letters. Several years ago they had fun with an overhead that had a picture of a cow. They made copies and let people create their own "cow" visuals. Examples included: "Cow-abunga" (cow on a surfboard) and "Cow-ard" (cow colored yellow).

▼ ▼ ▼

"I'm much more productive when I'm having fun. The work just flows."
—Sandy Tillotson, Training Coordinator

fun

A gain at Arthur Andersen, employees formed a group called the "Main Event Players" whose purpose is to renew and reenergize tax education personnel by providing opportunities for networking and social interaction. They plan three or four social events each year, which have been successful in the past with a high turnout. The group has enjoyed an annual holiday week, murder mystery parties, and trips to local sporting events.

▼ ▼ ▼

Dozens of top companies are finding that employees who laugh together stay together, produce more, invent more, and work more cohesively as a team.
—Bradford Swift, "HRMagazine," March 1994

teams

Initiations have long been used to build camaraderie and cohesiveness in organizations and on teams. As long as they are fun spirited and not mean spirited, work teams can also use an initiation to gain the benefits of a shared experience. The Cleveland Indians baseball team has a small initiation ritual for team newcomers. While the new player is watching the ball game from the bench, wily

pitcher Dennis Martinez will sneak up on the unsuspecting player and place a large bubblegum bubble on the very top of his baseball cap. Unfortunately for the new teammate, the unnoticed bubble will usually stay on top of the cap until the player's image is put up on the stadium Jumbotron or is picked up by a national television audience.

According to Jim Paluch, one of J.P. Horizons most popular seminars is the "Roundtable Olympics." The event, based on teams of people discussing important company issues, can be designed for groups as small as twenty or as large as three hundred. Each team is made up of individuals representing every facet of the company, who share ideas together and brainstorm plans of action. Tables are decorated with balloons, streamers, candy, bubble gum, and giant bowls of popcorn to add to the festive mood.

After each topic is discussed, the teams get up from their seats and compete in one of the Olympic events (basketball, football, golf, hockey, or pie throwing). The fun that participants have in alternating these events with the discussions of vital company topics helps everyone to develop camaraderie and wake up the right side of their brains, leading to valuable business input. A new dimension is added to the fun as each team works together to win the gold, silver, or bronze medals awarded at the end. As Jim says,

teams

"Something magical happens every time we do this seminar. It proves time and again that people do their best thinking when they are having fun, not when they are under pressure."

Whether it's throwing pies, showing *I Love Lucy* videos, sitting on beanbag chairs, painting pictures, using hula hoops, silly string, or confetti canons, people wake up by having fun and they learn, think, and perform more effectively.

"Fun is seeing tasks as challenges you can enjoy tackling."

—Stacy Yusim, Curriculum Developer, BOCA International, Inc.

B renda Paik Sunoo of *Personnel Journal* magazine writes in the June 1995 issue:

fun

"New hires at Southwest Airlines participate in an exercise designed to demonstrate creativity through teamwork. A team of eight is given twelve straws, four strips of masking tape, and a raw egg. The objective: to manufacture a device in seven minutes that will keep the egg intact when it's dropped from a height of ten feet. We roll out the plastic, and they have to test their device. There's exhilaration, disappointment, and everything in between."

After each team completes its experiment, the class listens to each team share how it devised its invention. Team success depends on the dynamics: how creative they wanted to be; whose idea they were willing to entertain; how they were able to identify and tap a member's expertise or ideas. "The most important lesson is forging teamwork with limited time constraints. There's always one successful team."

teams

A team I was working with recently requested that we maintain the ritual of ending every meeting on a positive note. In observance of their request, at the close of the meeting, I asked for ideas about how to end the session. A team member volunteered this exercise, which we did.

Everyone stood in a circle, holding hands if we wanted to. We were instructed to say the word "Ha!" continuously, out loud, for a full minute. Wow! I never thought that a minute could be *soooooo* long.

What happened was remarkable. Even the most serious in the group couldn't keep a straight face. The laughter grew louder and more raucous as the minute wore on.

We certainly departed in high spirits.

An interesting way to get your teams to think out of the box is to play a game similar to one that Gail Newman of American Management Systems has devised. During team training, she gives each team a series of cards with which to solve a "project management" puzzle. As the teams begin working on their project, it becomes evident that they do not have all the cards they need to solve the puzzle. Eventually one of the teams realizes that the solution can only be found by collaborating with the other teams in the training session. Gail finds that this is an excellent way to demonstrate both how to think creatively and how successful cross-functional teams work.

▼   ▼   ▼

The Pine Wood Derby, a model car race, has been a Cub Scout tradition for many years. The cars in a Pine Wood Derby are made by the Scouts from a block of wood. One Cub Scout district livened up its derby by inviting local engineering firms, universities, and even NASA to compete in a "Pine Wood Derby Corporate Challenge." The organizations involved created race teams that tried to create the perfect race car. The contest was a fun display of company pride and expertise. It also raised a good deal of money for the Cub Scouts.

teams

DAVE'S (HEMSATH)

TOP TEN LIST

of most recommended fun resource books (as compiled from our surveys):

10. "Nuts!"
 9. "Fax This Book!"
 8. "Lighten Up!"
 7. "1001 Ways to Reward Employees"
 6. "Great American Bathroom Book" (a wonderful all-purpose book)
 5. "Big Book of Business Games"
 4. "Managing to Have Fun"
 3. "Games Trainers Play" (series of four books)
 2. "Chicken Soup for the Soul" (books I, II, and III) and "Chicken Soup for the Soul at Work," and
#1. "The Dilbert Principle" (also "Dogbert's Top Secret Management Handbook")

Bank executives are typically a conservative and low-key group of people. A team of senior executives from Central Bank and Trust in Fort Worth, Texas, went a long way to dispel this stereotype one recent Halloween.

Many companies allow and even encourage their employees to dress up on Halloween. In some companies, executive-level management even participates. The Central Bank executives went one step further—their corporate headquarters sponsored a costume contest and awarded prizes to employees for special costumes at each of their twenty-six branches. Getting into the holiday spirit, a group of senior-level executives traveled from branch to branch to judge the costumes of the branch personnel. What made it particularly fun was the executives themselves were dressed as Olde English judges, complete with white wigs and robes. They enjoyed being out with their employees so much that they reportedly spent over two thousand dollars in prizes, giving awards to several people at each branch.

This was one Halloween those employees will never forget.

teams

"Humor ranks among the most powerful of management tools and serves many functions; it can be a coping mechanism, a negotiation facilitator, a communication instrument, a cognitive tool, a motivator, a creative force, a survival device, and much more."

—Frank Boruch, "HRMagazine," August 1995

▼   ▼   ▼

B illie Davis of Davis and Associates in Seattle, Washington, knows how hard it is to get uninterrupted time to spend with her team. She has found the best way to get away from all distractions is to take her team boating. Billie also mentions that in her office they give awards to those who made the biggest mistake in a given month. (I hope that doesn't mean the winners get to walk the plank.)

fun

athleen Fitzsimons of the Cleveland Clinic Foundation has found that hosting a product party, like a Longenberger Basket party, is a great way to create an environment that allows for a little silliness and playfulness in the workplace. Hosting a product party might be a great way to take a break from the typical lunchtime or after-work routine. You may even come home with a nice gift.

▼　　▼　　▼

"Creativity is allowing yourself to make mistakes. Art is knowing which ones to keep."
—Scott Adams, "The Dilbert Principle"

▼　　▼　　▼

iving your team a name is a popular way to build team spirit on and off the field. Elaine Hanna from MAMTC in Wichita, Kansas, says that team names at her office have developed such strong identities that team members are

teams

referred to as "Jane from the Slickers." Other clever team names we've seen are "69 Slide," "Stealth," and "The Clowns."

▼　　▼　　▼

K aiser Permanente announces recipients of work-group rewards at their division meetings. Winners are encouraged to spend their reward (one hundred dollars) as a group, doing something fun. Past winners have done things like buying box seats at an Oakland A's baseball game complete with food and drinks (taken during a work day), or taking a wine-train trip in the Napa Valley, with a gourmet lunch, also on a work day.

Kaiser also has a fun team-building activity that they do each December. One year during a division meeting, teams were formed, given the proper tools, and asked to build gingerbread hospitals and medical office buildings. This is exactly what these teams do on a daily basis in the real world. It was a nice diversion to do a complete project together in an edible world.

fun

Larry Dennis, president of Turbo Management Systems, fosters workplace fun by setting and stretching team sales goals. Larry writes: "Whenever we exceed our monthly goal, the entire sales team goes on a Friday afternoon outing. The sales associate who contributed most to that month's volume is the person who gets to plan the program. One of our outings was jet-skiing for the entire team, another was go-carting and putt-putt golfing, another was bowling, then a paint ball war, and still another was going to see the Great Wall of China exhibit. Each of these events is accompanied by food and has helped us feel closer to each other. One of the other secrets, of course, is to take plenty of pictures. Those fun memories then dwell in our minds so that we can recommit to stretching goals for the next month and quarter."

"Fun may not be measurable but it sure feels better."
    —Tim Ziska, Jr., Ziska Architects and Associates

teams

> **"Fun allows workers to risk without serious threat and to laugh at a situation that might otherwise be too serious."**
>
> **—Cyndi Maxey, Maxey Creative Inc.**

S ally Hudson recalls a fun ritual: "My father worked his whole career as a salesperson for a paper distributor. Every year the salespeople would divide into two teams and compete for the highest sales. In October they would tally the results and then gather for the annual Steak and Beans dinner. The winning team ate steak and the losing team ate beans. It was a wonderful ritual that incited friendly competition and became part of the lore of Fraser Paper Company."

▼　　▼　　▼

A sking for money can be intimidating. If you work for an organization that does fundraising you might take the "d," or "difficulty," out of fundraising and make it *fun*-raising instead.

fun

Your efforts to collect money for important causes can be enhanced through the use of fun. Asking isn't hard when you are involved in something you like. For example, create an event around the fund-raising activity: develop a theme, play bingo for donated prizes, throw a pizza or ice cream sundae party for departments that have 100 percent participation, hold a raffle that gives away valued company resources (free parking spots, extra vacation days, attendance at special events). The opportunities are infinite.

▼   ▼   ▼

Fun ideas for building teams are all around us. They come in the form of everyday-situation stories, art, music, and film. Incorporating these ideas into our activities stimulates renewed energy and a fresh perspective. It is also fun to break away. One of my favorite movie breaks is *Apollo 13*. The video is chock full of examples of successful team building, problem solving, and leadership.

teams

FUN FOCUS

BREWING FUN AT REDHOOK ALE BREWERY

Redhook Ale Brewery, which was founded in the early 1980s by Paul Shipman and Gordon Bowker (also the founder of Starbucks Coffee) in a small Seattle neighborhood, has found that fun comes as a result of valuing every individual's contributions to the success of the company. This empowering environment has created a lean, strong, and diverse workforce that has seen Redhook grow from a small, regional brewery to one with national distribution and huge annual increases in sales and production.

A HEAD FOR BUSINESS

From a modest production of 1,000 barrels in 1981, Redhook Ale Brewery has grown to be one of the most successful specialty breweries in the United States. Estimated production in 1996 should exceed 190,000 barrels. Redhook recently opened its third brewery, in Portsmouth, New Hampshire, to complement its two facilities in the state of Washington. The new brewery, along with a distribution arrangement with Anheuser-Busch, has assured the continued growth and nationwide distribution of Redhook products.

As a small, emerging business, Redhook had no preestablished cultural

fun

guidelines. Their culture has been developed primarily around individuals who have a passion for beer. This passion for the product has fostered an atmosphere of creativity and fun. In fact, many friends and family members regard Redhook employees as not even having jobs. They work for the love of beer.

As with many perceived "fun" companies, it may not be the specific things the company does so much as the larger organizational values that create a workplace considered to be fun by outsiders. Empowerment, open communication, employee interdependence, and trust are all contributing factors to the brewery being a fun place to work.

BEER AFICIONADOS

Redhook has created this culture by encouraging total employee participation in the growth of the business.

Redhook has approximately 260 full-time employees, but every person has an important role in promoting and selling Redhook beers. For starters, every employee is issued a business card, from sales and management personnel to staffers of the Forecasters Public House (a company pub at the Woodinville, Washington, brewery). This has created a sales and marketing team of 260 members who visit bars, supermarkets, and beverage stores to check on Redhook sales and get customer feedback. "We have a collective appreciation for looking at our products in public," says Nelson Jay of Redhook. "We always have our antennas up."

This collective appreciation spills over into the office environment. Employees are encouraged to exchange ideas openly between departments. The physical layout of the office is designed to give a newsroom

teams

feel, without doors or barriers that might inhibit the free flow of ideas. There is a real family feel to this company.

THE BREW TEAM

Redhook encourages the involvement of its employees in outside activities. There are several employee recreation teams within the company, but what makes Redhook unusual is their fun contributions, both financial and emotional, to these recreational teams and also to individual pursuits. It is common for a team to sport company T-shirts or to have a van load of coworkers come to cheer on an individual in a bike race, a marathon, or an ultimate Frisbee competition. Redhook feels that support for their employees doesn't end at the exits to their buildings.

Redhook team involvement includes participation in charity functions and beer festivals, common events throughout the year in Washington. All employees get an opportunity to staff one or more beer festivals or charity events, a perk typically given to marketing or public relations people at other breweries.

It could be said that Redhook has created fun activities for people outside the company as well. Redhook University was created to offer a wide variety of classes for beer enthusiasts and home brewers who want to learn more about how beer is made or how to improve their ability to create their own craft beer. For a nominal charge, employees and the public alike can have fun in a relaxed environment, meet people with similar interests, and expand their knowledge of brewing.

Redhook employees share a commitment to the success of their company, love of their product, dependence on their coworkers, and total enjoyment of their work: a perfect formula for a classic, fun workplace.

SIMPLE ACTS OF FUN

SIMPLE ACTS
OF FUN

Having fun at work should not be an
endless chore or a long list of things you must
do. That misses the point. Many things that
you and your coworkers can do to enliven your
workplace are simple, spontaneous acts.
Encouraging fun in your workplace doesn't
mean ignoring or neglecting organizational
objectives and becoming a frivolous time-
waster. Used effectively, fun can boost the
energy individuals have for their work,
resulting in improved performance.

Simple acts of fun are the large and
small things we do with our colleagues that
leave a memorable impression. They are the

seemingly insignificant things that make work fun—the sanity breaks, the times we stop and laugh, and especially the chances to be silly. In short, they **are** the reasons people like coming to work. Simple acts allow us to be childlike, to have fun for fun's sake.

Simple acts are quick and **easy** ways to put a charge in the energy level of your coworkers. Jump-start the level of fun in your workplace with a few of these great ideas.

Ben & Jerry's Homemade, Inc., started the Joy Gang, a committee that distributes joy grants to departments that come up with creative ways to bring happiness to the workplace. The grants can be used for anything—from purchasing a hot chocolate machine to hiring a masseuse for tired workers.

▼ ▼ ▼

Many offices have implemented a dress-down or casual-dress day. To add a fun twist to this tradition try a "dress-up" day. Halloween, Christmas, Thanksgiving are only some of the opportunities to dress the part for the day, building creativity and esprit de corps among employees. Banks, retail stores, even casinos have helped their customers have more fun by dressing up.

"Happiness rubs off on those around you."
—Sandy Tillotson, Training Coordinator

▼   ▼   ▼

Fun and productivity can go hand in hand. When you need to be left alone to get something accomplished, do what Stephen Datena of the Larrey Surgical Clinic in Portland, Oregon, does. He puts a "Go Away" doormat in front of his office door. Coworkers can borrow the mat when they need uninterrupted work time.

▼   ▼   ▼

Many companies use comics and comic strips as a way to bring perspective and levity to the workplace. Try including your favorite strip on interoffice mail, memos, and fax cover letters. The most popular strip? Dilbert of course.

acts

On casual-dress Fridays: "Work from the inside out and begin by appreciating that there is no point in putting on anything that makes you feel uneasy. Clothes are the easy part. Casual Friday winners will be known by the ease with which they display them."

—Robert Glasser, "Continental Magazine," November 1996

▼　　▼　　▼

Telling a joke can be an art form. It is fun to tell jokes and just as much fun to be told a joke. A fun way to maintain healthy relationships is to share a joke or two. Scott, a maintenance employee in our building, is the Johnny Appleseed of joke telling. As he makes his way through the building each day, he stops frequently in offices to plant the seed of his newest joke. This quick break is a pleasant diversion from the daily demands of work. We have come to look forward to his happy

simple

interruptions, which have created friendly relationships with all the tenants and set a tone and tenor throughout the building that is warm and welcoming. Thank you, Scott.

▼   ▼   ▼

A well-developed sense of humor helps relieve tension and reduce stress. One way to help develop a sense of humor and fun in your coworkers is to leave joke books, humor books, or cartoon books, such as *The Far Side, Dilbert,* or *Calvin and Hobbes* in the lunchroom.

▼   ▼   ▼

H elp coworkers develop their humor skills by encouraging them to share funny incidents and stories. The grapevine can sometimes be a more effective source of information in organizations than the more formal vehicles. Kathleen Unland and Dr. Brian Kleiner of California State University at Fullerton

acts

urge individuals to cultivate their sense of humor; they teach people to take themselves lightly while taking their jobs seriously. They understand the power of good news traveling fast and prompt everyone to tell stories about positive and funny situations at work, focusing less on the negative.

A s part of your effort to develop your skills and talents for creating fun, look for inspiration in others. Many skills and techniques can be learned by observing others. Find someone to be your "Humor Hero" or "Fun Friend."

"Fun means enjoying coming to work, smiling about being there, and most importantly, making sure that the job gets done."
—Jerry Kaminski, Director of Staff Development, Wayne County, Michigan

simple

C reate a fun file. Capture fun ideas and humorous resources in a file filled with newspaper clippings, cartoons, and headlines. Expand your file to be a "fun first-aid kit," with objects that stimulate laughter and create fun breaks. Before you know it, you will have a fun drawer bulging with ideas and activities to keep the joy in work.

▼   ▼   ▼

A new tradition is beginning—one day during the year working mothers are bringing their daughters to work. The idea is to give young women a new perspective on working women and positive role models. I would like to see this tradition expanded to include all children and all parents. Some businesses have already started "Children's Day," modeled after the common practice of Parents' Day at many colleges and universities. A parent brings a child (or children) to work and shows them where they

acts

work, what they do, with whom they work. Many parents gain renewed interest and pride in their work when they have an opportunity to share with their children. There is a wonderful secondary benefit to this practice—nothing motivates me more to clear my desk than knowing my children are coming for a visit.

When things seem to be going from bad to worse, take a time out. Put whatever is happening into perspective—create your own personalized "Murphy's Laws."

▼ ▼ ▼

In its March 1994 issue, *HRMagazine* reports that some companies have changed their "sick room" to a humor room, filling it with puzzles, comic books, games, and toys, so harried employees can slip away on a break for a few minutes of "en-lighten-ment."

simple

A restaurant in Oakland, California, hosts an annual napkin decorating contest for all its patrons. The contest generates a lot of enthusiasm for both the customers and the restaurant staff. The winner of the contest receives a nice prize and all of the entries are used to decorate the restaurant. It is a great way to increase repeat business as all the budding napkin artists bring their friends and relatives back to view their entries.

One Arthur Andersen office hosts a "Baby-Day Lunch" once a month. It is an opportunity for mothers to bring their babies, show them off, and talk about Mommy stuff, parenting, and so on.

acts

nother Arthur Andersen office has hung several white boards throughout their facility that are used for the "Questions of the Month." For example: What good movies have you seen lately? What is your favorite song from the seventies? If you could take one thing back to the year 1850, what would it be? If you had the chance to name a new Crayola Crayon color, what would it be? What is your favorite childhood memory? And the list goes on.

▼　　▼　　▼

ngineers at Sun Microsystems play elaborate April Fools' Day jokes on company executives. Past pranks have included turning the CEO's office into a miniature golf course and putting the cofounders Ferrari in the middle of a fish pond. Surprisingly, the executives encourage the gags. The pranks are videotaped to show employees at other sites, and T-shirts are sold to commemorate, and fund, the event.

simple

merica has been taken by storm with a song and an easy to learn dance to accompany the music. You can't go anywhere without hearing the beat of the Macarena. Suddenly people of all ages, races, genders, even the New York Yankees ground crew are joining together to dance to this catchy tune. It has even invaded the workplace. I have seen spontaneous groups of employees stop their work for a quick session of the Macarena.

▼　▼　▼

ake advantage of holidays, especially the holiday created for fun, April Fool's Day. At an Arthur Andersen office they have fun with April Fool's Day pranks by mixing up the desktops of colleagues and replacing favorite family photos with new ones, or even turning everything in the office upside down. Of course, it is all temporary and done in the spirit of fun.

acts

A̲ t Cambria Consulting an employee suggested something fun . . . sponsor a "polka-dot day." All employees were encouraged to wear polka-dotted clothing. Many employees participated, dressing head to toe in dots.

D̲ uring a particularly stressful time while working on the annual budget, Denise Dakis of United Airlines found a fun way to keep her spirits high. She stuck positive affirmations written on Post-it notes all around her desk, her computer, and her cubicle. Whenever she started feeling low, a funny saying or joke was always within view. The notes were so effective that Denise's coworkers got into the act by placing notes in all the budget coordinators offices to help lighten their budgetary load.

simple

According to the "Wall Street Journal" (January 21, 1997), the trend toward business casual clothing continues to spread, but the casual pendulum may have swung too far. Many professionals have taken casual attire to an inappropriate level, and men seem to be the biggest culprits. Hal Lancaster suggests this quick guide to dressing casual while still looking like you mean business:

1. Acceptable casual wear generally consists of natural-fiber slacks, a dressy, casual shirt, a blazer, and high-end loafers.
2. Avoid golf pants, jeans, warm-up suits, and T-shirts.
3. When in doubt, mimic the boss.

▼　　▼　　▼

An idea from *HRMagazine*, March 1994: Create humor boards. Designate certain bulletin boards or sections of boards for humor pieces, cartoons, jokes, funny sayings.

acts

DAVE'S (HEMSATH)

TOP TEN LIST

of most popular office toys (as compiled from our surveys):

10. **Pogo Sticks or Hula Hoops**
9. **Yo Yos**
8. **Tinkertoys**
7. **Slinky**
6. **Pez dispensers**
5. **Frisbees (or Roomarangs)**
4. **Silly Putty**
3. **Nerf Balls**
2. **Nerf Guns, and**
#1. **Koosh Balls**

▼   ▼   ▼

S teve Cardamone of BOCA International puts new meaning into the phrase "hit and run." As a funmeister par excellence, he chooses to think of his life's modus operandi as "just smile and run!"

simple

Gifts are always nice to give and receive. Gifts can also be a fun way to build relationships with clients or coworkers. Chip Bell, author of several books on management and customer service, is distinctly proud of being a Texan. On many trips, Chip has been known to come bearing gifts of hats, T-shirts, and books proclaiming the greatness of the state of Texas. These gifts have always been received with thanks and good cheer, but on a recent visit to his publisher in San Francisco he may have gone too far. He presented each staff member with a Dallas Cowboys bumper sticker. The Cowboys are arch rivals of the very popular San Francisco Forty-Niners. The stickers were refused.

▼　　▼　　▼

"We look for attitudes: people with a sense of humor who don't take themselves too seriously. We'll train people on whatever it is they need to do, but the one thing Southwest cannot change in people is inherent attitudes."

—Herb Kelleher, CEO Southwest Airlines

acts

B J Hateley, consultant and author of the bestselling book *A Peacock in the Land of Penguins*, gives the following advice:

F requently read a few pages of this book.

U nlimited productivity potential.

N ew solutions to old problems.

A ppoint a vice president of fun where you work.

T ry at least one idea from this book every week.

W ork and play, simultaneously.

O rganize a Fun Squad to continuously look for new ways to make work fun.

R eward fun ideas, projects, and activities that make work a better place to be.

K ick yourself in the butt if you ever stop having fun.

simple

200

Anna Kochka, human resource manager of Nokia Mobile Phones in San Diego, California, mentions one of the companies most successful "work must be fun" applications. "We sponsor an all-employee band. Once per quarter we have a Nokia band happy hour. Members of the band include senior project managers and technicians as well as secretaries." On a different note, Anna goes on to say, "We give all employees the responsibility to shape our culture and work environment. They are empowered to create the environment they want to have."

Sounds like this workplace not only carries fun to a high level, but they can also carry a tune!

Holly Halvorson from Colorado Trust in Denver strongly believes that fun is one of the most critical aspects for her and her work. One time, to make sure that she didn't forget the importance of having fun at work, she penciled the word "Fun" into the doorway where she could see it for a constant reminder.

acts

Holly's simple rules for keeping a fun attitude on a daily basis:

- ▼ Inject self-deprecation into every conversation, so that laughter starts with yourself.
- ▼ Play with words instead of people.
- ▼ Encourage people to laugh at their mistakes.
- ▼ Promote telling success stories, no matter how small.

Holly is a great model for anyone wanting to put more fun into their work. She realizes that it is the small things done on a daily basis that create an environment that fosters teamwork, creativity, and productivity. From the simple act of whistling to laughing out loud, Holly calls upon her own internal energy to create more fun for everyone. "I infuse *fun* into everything I do. Otherwise, what's the purpose?"

simple

The March 1994 issue of *HRMagazine* mentions that a favorite idea of Matt Weinstein, president of Playfair, Inc., is to pass out stress support kits. His stress support kit includes wind-up teeth for a busy executive to play with when stuck on a particularly boring phone call, a red clown nose to wear during traffic jams, and pens that look like vegetables.

▼   ▼   ▼

Many companies are using email for fun communication and camaraderie. One company has a self-proclaimed keeper of the bottomless candy jar, who likes to use email to keep the office informed of new candy arrivals. Email has become a virtual gathering place for many offices.

▼   ▼   ▼

"Work is not a curse, but drudgery is."

—Henry Ward Beecher

acts

he popularity of disposable cameras has made it possible not only to catch a "Kodak" moment but also to create some of your own. OptimalCare in Phoenix, Arizona, likes to keep a camera on hand for photo opportunities as they occur. Most pictures are taken when the staff is playing or having fun, so once the photos have been developed and posted, they become great reminders of those fun times.

▼　　▼　　▼

lways try to make fun a priority and don't postpone your fun. Leonard Agosta of RWD Technologies enjoys his work so much that he tries not to let anything distract him from it. He uses prioritization and focus to continue doing the things that create for him the most joy: successful completion of his projects. Leonard feels that his fun/work focus allows his brain to continue to problem solve and address business issues even after business hours.

TO DO:
1) HAVE FUN!
2) LIGHTEN UP!

simple

Tickle Me Elmo is a fun children's toy that can bring a lot of smiles to the office. Elmo, a popular Muppett character, laughs hysterically when you tickle him, and the laughter is definitely contagious.

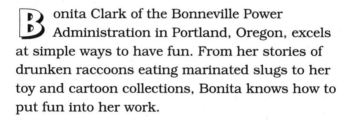

▼   ▼   ▼

Bonita Clark of the Bonneville Power Administration in Portland, Oregon, excels at simple ways to have fun. From her stories of drunken raccoons eating marinated slugs to her toy and cartoon collections, Bonita knows how to put fun into her work.

To spice up her workday, Bonita says: "I look at my *Why Cats Paint* book, I do cartwheels every now and then, I leave a beautiful autumn leaf on someone's desk, I tickle people (only those I know won't file a lawsuit), I turn on my dancing penguin, I take myself lightly, and I smile a big smile and say hello to people I don't know."

Bonita knows that it isn't only the big things you do that make work fun, it is the small things you do every day that bring a smile to your coworker's face . . . and mine.

acts

> **"Fun at work means enjoying what you do so much that the weekends come too soon."**
> **—Del Rae Grose, Roberts Express Trucking Company**

▼　▼　▼

GTE Data Services is another fun company. Their simple acts include pizza lunches for departments; sundae workdays, where management, decked out in chef hats, serves up the ice cream; and team yo-yos emblazoned with the company logo and the slogan, "Work has its ups and downs."

▼　▼　▼

Create your own personal book of fun and inspirational quotes.

Rhonda Wiley-Jones, a human resource specialist from Iowa State University, has a blank journal that she keeps at her desk. When she finds a quote or saying she likes, it goes into the journal. Rhonda writes each entry in a different colored ink and can get six to eight quotes per page. When she goes back to look through her journal, she finds a colorful mosaic of inspirational quotes that never fails to give her a lift.

▼   ▼   ▼

"A fun workplace makes my one and one-half hour commute worthwhile."
—Dianna Wilusz, National Semiconductor

▼   ▼   ▼

C arolyne Check, system director for human resources development at HealthEast in St. Paul, Minnesota, has helped to create a tremendously fun workplace. Following are some of her simple acts:
▼ She encourages office toys. A favorite is a magnetic paper-doll collection with dozens of outfits that lives on a filing cabinet in her

acts

office. People know it is there, and they stop by frequently to dress both David and Venus in crazy combinations of clothes.

▼ They send teams of people to "Glamour Shots" together to have group photos done wearing feather boas.

▼ They planted pots of spring bulbs together in the fall so everyone could have flowers bloom this winter in their offices.

▼ They try to do the unexpected instead of following the norm. For example, a presentation on the future of the business was not the standard boring speeches and slides. They shot a totally hilarious video starring employees. It was done as a spoof on *Entertainment Tonight.* That got people's attention—right up to the CEO.

Carolyne really knows how to add fun to everything she does.

▼   ▼   ▼

"In a fun workplace, problems are handled with consideration."

—Anonymous

simple

ngela Gann, a manager for the National Facilities Services division of Kaiser Permanente in Oakland, California, developed several fun rituals for her office. At their annual holiday party, they auction off their managers to the highest bidder. All the money raised goes into their community fund and is distributed to several organizations for their annual food drives. The auction winner gets to use the manager for four hours of slave labor. Angela's office has raised over five hundred dollars each time they have held the auction. Angela says, "One of our favorite pastimes is making fun of the boss. He loves it too. We are into torture and torment . . . keeps people on their toes."

In addition, Angela Gann and her coworkers at Kaiser Permanente sometimes gather at lunch for dramatic readings of the local newspaper. This lunchtime event usually happens when times have been particularly stressful.

acts

Sally J. Hudson of Bank of America keeps a supply of coworker "head shots" (passport photos work great) on hand so that she can paste a familiar head onto a different body. Sally writes: "I used to collect various magazine photos for this. A famous choral group became the bodies for our heads for a team promotion; my boss's head ended up on a champion boxer's body to show what a champ he was. The two partners in our group turned into Santa and his helper on our Christmas party invitation one year."

▼　　▼　　▼

Jim Paluch of J.P. Horizons, Inc., tells us that smiling is the universal act of openness and friendship. Following are a few smiling facts:

▼ Smiling makes you happier—the facial muscles you move actually send messages back to the brain changing your emotional state for the better.
▼ Women smile eight more times than men throughout the day. Interestingly, women live

simple

eight years longer on average than men; that's one year for every grin.

▼ People like and trust you more if you smile. Smiling is a cue to openness and acceptance. Make a real commitment and show some teeth!

▼ People can hear you smile. A listener doesn't have to see you to know that you're smiling, it is conveyed in the tone of your voice.

▼ Smiling actually cools the brain while frowning heats it up. A Stanford University study showed that blood supply to the brain is cooled by the facial movements and breathing patterns of smiling; the contracted muscles of frowning do the opposite.

▼ ▼ ▼

The sales director of a large New York corporation hired a theater director to teach his salesmen to smile. Sales went up 15 percent within three months of the lessons.

FACTS

—Seth Godin, "Wisdom Inc."

acts

*S*ally J. Hudson of Bank of America fondly remembers her former boss, Bob Waterman, coauthor of *In Search of Excellence,* for his love of movies. Sally recalls that "on occasion, he'd round us all up to go to an afternoon matinee. Same for early spring days. He'd decide we really should be out enjoying the sunshine and send us all home."

▼   ▼   ▼

*Y*our work day starts before you even hit the office. David Bryson suggests incorporating the following ideas into your daily commute:

▼ Buy a funky-looking pair of sunglasses that you would never wear anywhere else but in traffic. It's fun to see the reactions of fellow commuters as you drive by.

▼ Rent a book-on-tape for a long drive.

▼ A friend of David's in Charlotte, North Carolina, created a "Commute Butt-Burn" audiotape that you can use while sitting in your car.

simple

FUN FOCUS

FUN IS THE NAME OF THE GAME AT SHOWTIME NETWORKS

Showtime Networks, Inc., a premium cable television channel, has made fun a key sales and customer service strategy for its regional sales offices, successfully differentiating itself in the crowded cable television industry. This strategy has also resulted in a fun office environment, which has brought the company a low rate of turnover and a high standard of excellence.

BROADCASTING FUN

Showtime Networks supports eight regional sales offices, which are responsible for sales and distribution to cable television providers. The account representatives in these offices handle sales calls, service accounts, train the frontline cable television sales representatives in the Showtime product, and entertain key clients. Because they are selling entertainment, Showtime account reps have taken on a role that many cable system employees see as fun and exciting. Showtime reps routinely show up for product training in costume and often include games in their training efforts. Interaction and involvement are central to successful Showtime training. The Showtime reps have found that the key to their success is the value they place on humor, fun, and relationships in all their business dealings.

The lessons learned by the reps have penetrated the entire organization. Regional and companywide meetings now routinely involve skits, jokes, storytelling, music, and theatrics. This company culture does, however, have its roots in a conscious business strategy.

In the relatively new and fast-growing cable television industry of the early 1980s, Showtime started out as a distant second-place competitor to the industry leader, Home Box Office (HBO), which had a lock on distribution and sales. But cable system employees viewed the HBO sales reps as inflexible and unexciting. Showtime recognized that if they could develop relationships with the frontline marketing and point of sales cable employees, who had largely been ignored by their bigger competitor, they could take advantage of a tremendous business opportunity. They accomplished this

goal by having fun with cable employees. Games, entertainment, skits, and warm relationships have become hallmarks of Showtime's sales and marketing efforts. The strategy has paid off as Showtime has grown exponentially over the last ten years and has become widely recognized and respected in the cable industry for valuing fun and humor in the workplace.

WHAT'S IN A NAME

At Showtime's small satellite office in San Francisco, the culture of fun and humor has developed side by side with a strong work ethic and a high standard of excellence.

One of their fun rituals is to give everybody a new name. It started like this: A few years back during an especially stressful time, the staff decided to hold a party every couple of weeks to help build team morale and pride, as well as to

simple

blow off a little steam. At one party there were twenty or more people, so no one knew everyone's name. Someone made up names that seemed to fit for two people they didn't know (Luther and Kendra), and shortly thereafter, everyone was getting new names.

The Showtime people kept their new names and a tradition was born. Now, every time the office staff gets together for holiday parties, summer picnics, or office meetings, if there is a newcomer, they get a new name. Sometimes even visitors to the office, who happen to attend company gatherings, get names. No one has been left out.

The rules have developed with the process. For example, the person being named has no say in picking their new name, unless they show distaste for a suggested name, in which case it automatically sticks. The group may ask the initiate

about events in their childhood, or a name may be suggested by how the person looks (or doesn't look).

At some point over the years, people began to be officially "knighted" with their new names at company dinners. A fork tap on each shoulder and one on top of the head officially proclaimed "Sir Loin of Beef," "Sir Ossis of the Liver," or "Count of Basie." On one canoe outing, the names were proclaimed in drenched bathing suits with a canoe paddle.

For this Showtime office, fun has become one of the most productive uses of their workplace energy. They have found that spontaneous fun— the type that happens because you care about the people you work with or the people you serve as customers—is enlivening and energizing.

acts

A TWELVE-STEP METHOD TO FUN

Fun is a simple phenomenon—anyone can participate. Fun doesn't require special training, it won't necessarily cost you money, and the benefits are infinite. Plus . . . it can have a positive impact on the lives of the people you work with every day.

Following is our twelve-step program for fun. We recommend that you read it daily, poke fun at yourself frequently, and perhaps commit to implementing one step a month for an entire year.

Feel free to post our illustrations and prescriptions liberally around your office. Remember: It's a fun world after all!

twelve steps to fun

1. **Start with Yourself**

2. **Inspire Fun in Others**

3. **Create an Environment That Encourages Fun**

4. **Celebrate the Benefits of Fun**

5. **Eliminate Boundaries and Obstacles That Inhibit Fun**

6. **Look for the Humor in Your Situation**

7. **Follow Your Intuition—Be Spontaneous**

8. **Don't Postpone Your Fun**

9. **Make Fun Inclusive**

10. **Smile and Laugh a Lot**

11. **Become Known as "Fun Loving"**

12. **Put Fun into Action**

1

START WITH YOURSELF

▼ Don't wait for someone
  else to start the fun—
  become the fun catalyst.

▼ Discover the fun that naturally resides within you. Examine how
  you spend your time and evaluate what you can change to
  enliven the spontaneous, fun spirit within yourself and your
  coworkers.

▼ Each of us is fun in our own unique way. Cultivate your natural
  style. Get a little zany and create a chain reaction of frivolity that
  starts with you.

"All I wanna do is have some fun.
I got a feeling I'm not the only one."

—Sherly Crow, A&M recording artist

INSPIRE FUN IN OTHERS

▼ Be a role model for fun. Encourage others to engage in fun-loving activities. Recognize and support the effort of others in the creation of fun.

▼ Take risks. Don't be afraid to appear silly.

▼ Give gifts that will stimulate fun and spontaneity.

"Remind yourself that the simplest things in life yield the greatest dividends."

—Bryan E. Robinson, Ph.D.

3

CREATE AN ENVIRONMENT THAT ENCOURAGES FUN

▼ The environment in which we work can have a great impact on our attitude. Choose colors that enliven your spirit, use music to brighten your mood, and have toys within reach to relieve stress.

▼ Surprise yourself and others by changing things around regularly.

"Laughter is the shortest distance between two people."

—Victor Borge

CELEBRATE THE BENEFITS OF FUN

FUN = PRODUCTIVITY = PROFITS = GROWTH = MORE FUN = MORE PRODUCTIVITY...

▼ **Become fanatical about recognizing fun when you see it. Champion the cause of fun efforts and their benefits passionately. Take time to acknowledge your own and others' efforts to create a positive work environment for all.**

▼ **Be open to others' ideas about building a workplace that everyone enjoys and where all contribute to the fun.**

▼ **Use fun as an excuse to take a break and spontaneously celebrate good work and good effort.**

"Work hard and smart, but have fun as well. The more fun you have the more productive you will be."

—Abe Bakhsheshy, University of Utah Hospital

5

ELIMINATE BOUNDARIES AND OBSTACLES THAT INHIBIT FUN

▼ Fun is contagious and electric. Once unbridled, it will travel fast throughout an organization giving life and energy to all.

▼ Make it a goal to find and remove obstacles that inhibit the free flow of fun. Don't be afraid to confront those who discourage fun.

"If you obey all the rules, you miss all the fun."

—Katharine Hepburn

LOOK FOR THE HUMOR IN YOUR SITUATION

▼ There is a silver lining in every cloud. How hard are you prepared to look for it? People generally want to be around someone who is fun and optimistic rather than those who preach doom and gloom.

▼ Be the person who can find fun and humor in every situation. Always be ready to laugh, especially at yourself.

"Humor is an affirmation of dignity, a declaration of man's superiority to all that befalls him."

—Romain Gary

7

FOLLOW YOUR INTUITION —BE SPONTANEOUS

▼ **There is no appropriate time or place for fun. Don't wait for it to find you—make it occur whenever you need the boost.**

▼ **Use the elements of surprise and spontaneity to refresh your work and work relationships.**

"A person will be just about as happy as they make up their minds to be."

—Abraham Lincoln

DON'T POSTPONE YOUR FUN

▼ **Don't procrastinate or postpone having fun. Fun is not a reward for completing an assignment. It is the lubricant for getting things done well and working effectively with others. Make it a part of your daily routine.**

"Life is short. Live it up!"
—Nikita Khrushchev

MAKE FUN INCLUSIVE

▼ **Fun is for sharing. The moment that you exclude another from the fun it stops being fun.**

▼ **The more the merrier is the best attitude to adopt.**

"Treat people as if they were what they ought to be, and you help them to become what they are capable of being."

—Goethe

#

AND LAUGH A LOT

▼ Smiling and laughing cost nothing, they need no special skills, and take virtually no time to accomplish. Yet a smile or laugh can be the most positively contagious thing.

▼ Greet everyone with a smile, take the time for a hearty belly laugh at a joke or even at yourself. You will find others eager to join in the fun.

"Start every day off with a smile and get it over with."

—W. C. Fields

BECOME KNOWN AS "FUN LOVING"

▼ The greatest compliment you can receive is to be known as fun loving. Make it a personal mission to infuse fun into everything you do. Share your fun generously with others and let it light up your life.

"Choose a job you love, and you will never have to work a day in your life."

—Confucius

12

PUT FUN INTO ACTION

▼ Grab a fun idea and take action. One a day will keep your life filled with fun. Share ideas, borrow ideas, or create your own, but most importantly start now.

▼ Momentum and strength will come as a result of doing even the littlest thing everyday.

"He deserves Paradise who makes his companions laugh."

—The Koran

SUGGESTED READINGS

Adams, Scott. *The Dilbert Principle*. New York: HarperCollins, 1996.

Adams, Scott. *Dogbert's Top Secret Management Handbook*. New York: HarperCollins, 1996.

Anderson, Steven, ed. *The Great American Bathroom Book: Single Sitting Summaries of All-Time Great Books*. Salt Lake City: Compact Classics, 1994.

Blanchard, Kenneth, John P. Carlos, and Alan Randolph. *Empowerement Takes More Than a Minute*. San Francisco: Berrett-Koehler Publishers, 1996.

Byham, William C. *Zapp!: The Lightning of Empowerment*. New York: Fawcett Books, 1992.

Caldwell, John. *Fax This Book!* New York: Workman Publishing, 1990.

Canfield, Jack, and Mark Victor Hanson. *Chicken Soup for the Soul: 101 Stories to Open the Heart and Rekindle the Spirit*. Dearfiled Beach, Fla,: Health Communications, 1995.

Chapman, Elwood. *Life Is an Attitude*. San Diego, Ca.: Crisp Publications, 1992.

Collins, James, and Jerry Porras. *Built to Last*. New York: HarperCollins, 1994.

DeBono, Edward. *Six Thinking Hats*. International Center for Creative Thinking, 1988.

Foster, Jack. *How to Get Ideas*. San Francisco: Berrett-Koehler Publishers, 1996.

Freiberg, Kevin, and Jackie Freiberg. *Nuts!: Southwest Airlines' Crazy Recipe for Business and Personal Success.* Austin, Tx.: Bard Books, 1996.

Fulghum, Robert. *All I Really Need to Know I Learned in Kindergarten.* New York: Villard Books, 1986.

Kao, John J. *Jamming: The Art and Discipline of Business Creativity.* New York: HarperCollins, 1996.

Leider, Richard, and David Shapiro. *Repacking Your Bags: Lighten Your Load for the Rest of Your Life.* San Francisco: Berrett-Koehler Publishers, 1995.

McGee-Cooper, Ann. *You Don't Have to Go to Bed Exhausted.* New York: Brown and Rogers, 1990

McGinnis, Alan Loy. *Power of Optimism.* New York: Harper and Row, 1990.

Metcalf, C. W. *Lighten Up: Survival Skills for People under Pressure.* Reading, Mass.: Addison-Wesley Publishing, 1992.

Nelson, Bob. *1001 Ways to Reward Employees.* New York: Workman Publishing, 1994.

Newstrom, John, and Edward Scannell. *Big Book of Business Games: Icebreakers and Creativity Exercises.* New York: McGraw-Hill, 1995.

Newstrom, John, and Edward Scannell. *Games Trainers Play.* New York: McGraw-Hill, 1980.

Newstrom, John, and Edward Scannell. *More Games Trainers Play.* New York: McGraw-Hill, 1983.

Newstrom, John, and Edward Scannell. *Still More Games Trainers Play.* New York: McGraw-Hill, 1991.

Newstrom, John, and Edward Scannell. *Even More Games Trainers Play.* New York: McGraw-Hill, 1994.

Paulson, Terry L. *Making Humor Work.* San Diego, Ca.: Crisp Publications, 1989.

Popcorn, Faith. *The Popcorn Report: Faith Popcorn on the Future of Your Company.* New York: HarperCollins, 1992.

Popcorn, Faith, and Lys Marigold. *Clicking: 16 Trends to Future Fit Your Life, Your Work, and Your Business.* New York: HarperCollins, 1996.

Richards, Dick. *Artful Work: Awakening Joy, Meaning, and Commitment in the Workplace.* San Francisco: Berrett-Koehler Publishers, 1995.

Sanitate, Frank. *Don't Go to Work: Unless It's Fun.* Santa Barbara, Ca.: Santa Barbara Press, 1994.

von Oech, Roger. *A Whack on the Side of the Head.* New York: Warner Books, 1993.

Weinstein, Matt. *Managing to Have Fun.* New York: Simon and Schuster, 1996.

Wheatley, Margaret, and Myron Kellner-Rogers. *A Simpler Way.* San Francisco: Berrett-Koehler Publishers, 1996.

INDEX

Adams, Scott, 27, 175
affirmations, posting, 196
art
    display, 14, 40
    quilt making, 82, 89
    rainbow mosaic, 84-85
    wall of fame, 139-140
    See also drawing
attendance, 130
awards and certificates
    banner, 140-141
    ceremonies, 142, 145
    for mistakes, 174
    for vacation coverage, 131
    gift certificates, 20, 137
    health spa certificates, 144
    humorous, 116-117, 146
    mock, 15
    "well-day" cards, 130
    See also gifts; recognition;
        rewards
behaviorism, 130
Big Book of Business Games, 77
birthdays, 68, 136, 145, 149
books
    humorous, 27, 47, 134, 189,
        205
    on-tape, 212
    resource (top ten list), 172
brainstorming, 167-168
buddy system, 92-93
Canfield, Jack, 134
cartoons, 29, 152, 187, 189
    See also Dilbert

children in the workplace, 20-21,
    191-192, 193
Cleese, John, 108
Clicking, 26
communication, 44-45
    humorous, 46, 47, 48-49, 63-
      64
    on paycheck stubs, 138-139
    show-and-tell, 105
    storytelling, 189-190
Creative Whacks, 64
creativity, 76, 88-89, 104, 175
customer service
    improvements in, 19-20, 30-
      31, 61
    improving morale, 27-28
DeBono, Edward, 117-118
Dilbert, 5, 27, 61, 103, 187, 189
drawing, 13, 88-89
    blank chart paper for, 29
    contests, 141, 193
    See also art
dress
    casual, 15, 28, 40, 188, 197
    costumes, 28, 29, 186, 212
    hats, 16, 117-118, 119, 148
    lapel pins, 18
    polka-dot day, 196
    uniforms, 74-75
email, 57, 59, 203
employee needs, ranked, 37-38
food. *See* refreshments
Fridays, 6, 15
    See also dress, casual
Fulghum, Robert, 134
fun, 184-185
    collecting ideas, 191, 206-207

course completion party, 151-152

game books for trainers, 77

humorous slides, 87

organizing symposiums, 79-80

orientation ideas, 67-68, 77-78, 84-85, 90-91, 92-93

See also games

Twelve-Step Method to Fun, 216-229

"Uh-Oh Squad," 162-163

video-making, 208

voice mail, 22, 46, 59

von Oech, Roger, 64

weather, 4-5

Whack on the Side of the Head, A, 64

work environment

  break room, 192

  flexible, 6, 15

  fun, 2-3

  quiet, 26, 187

  wacky hour, 24

yoga, 89

COMPANIES FEATURED

AES Corp., 138

AGI, Inc., 114-115

Alltel Corporate Services, 101

American Management Systems, 86, 170-171

American Media, 91

Amy's Ice Cream, 30-31, 65

Animation, U.S.A., 152

Arthur Andersen, 106, 138, 164, 165, 193, 194

Augusta Technical Institute, 84-85

Austin, Texas (city of), 147

Avery Dennison, 17

Bank of America, 210, 212

Ben & Jerry's Homemade, Inc., 186

Berkeley Systems, 33

Berrett-Koehler Publishers, 105

Blonder Company, 19

BOCA International, 79-80, 168, 198

Bonneville Power Administration, 63, 205

Bradleylew, Inc., 58

Brew City, 160

Burke Marketing Research, 144

California State University, Fullerton, 189-190

Cambria Consulting, 109, 196

Capital One Services, 29, 149

CDA Management Consulting, Inc., 20-21

ABOUT THE AUTHORS

DAVE HEMSATH

Dave Hemsath is co-owner and founder of Business Outreach Books in Cleveland, Ohio. He is famous for implementing several of the fun ideas contained in this book in his own office as well as in the offices of his customers and suppliers. Some of his favorite fun ideas involve food (belly-buster taco pizza), drink (beer), and music (rock and roll) to loosen up a stressful workplace. He feels strongly that if you are not truly enjoying your work, you should find something else to do.

In the early 1990s, Dave actually walked his talk regarding finding something else. After spending several successful years working for a Fortune 500 chemical company, he left corporate America to strike out on his own, starting a manufacturer's rep firm. Dave was successful as a sales agent, winning several personal sales awards and an award for sales agency of the year. Unfortunately, he found that a life-long career demonstrating brooms and toilet bowl cleaners did not appeal to him.

So, following his love of books, Dave and his partner, Patrick McGovern, started Business Outreach Books in 1993. It has made all the difference in the world for him. Doing what he loves to do has unleashed his energy and creativity in a way that cannot be achieved when work becomes drudgery.

Dave graduated from Ohio State University with degrees in marketing and production management. His extensive experience in sales and marketing has brought him opportunities to teach at Cleveland-area high schools and Virginia Marti College. He occasionally speaks to community groups and associations, and has addressed many small business groups on entrepreneurship issues. Dave has written book reviews for many trade publications and newspapers and is currently working on his next book project, which deals with the challenges that face parents whose work involves a good deal of traveling.

Dave lives in Strongsville, Ohio, with his wife, Gayle, and two boys, Michael and Derek. In his spare time, Dave likes helping out with both of his sons' Cub Scout dens, coaching Little League baseball, watching the Cleveland Indians play baseball, and, of course, reading.

Dave Hemsath can be contacted at hemsath@msn.com, or at:

Business Outreach Books
1108 Chester Avenue
Cleveland, OH 44114
Tel: 216-348-1744
Fax: 216-348-0375

BUSINESS OUTREACH BOOKS

Business Outreach Books is the nation's largest operator of on-site bookstores for associations, conferences, seminars, and expositions. This unique bookselling niche was developed by founders and co-owners Dave Hemsath and Patrick McGovern. In the past five years, Business Outreach has facilitated over five hundred on-site bookstores and book tables, primarily at business and computer-related professional meetings.

Besides on-site bookstores, Business Outreach specializes in three areas that allow easy access to books for business professionals.

1. Business Outreach creates strategic partnerships with associations and Fortune 500 companies to facilitate ongoing book fulfillment programs. Business Outreach can be counted on to supply association members and corporate employees with the latest resources available.

2. Business Outreach maintains a database in excess of 100,000 names of business professionals who take advantage of special book pricing and other promotions made available to them through Business Outreach's biannual business and computer book catalog.

3. Business Outreach maintains a web site (www.bizoutreach.com) for those professionals who need specific information about the newest business

titles. Each title shows the book's table of contents, author biographies, an abstract, and the book jacket.

Business Outreach is headquartered in Cleveland, Ohio, with regional offices in Los Angeles and Atlanta. To contact Business Outreach Books or to request a catalog, call 800-968-9622 or email us at bizinfo@bizoutreach.com.

LESLIE YERKES

Leslie specializes in helping organizations turn challenges into opportunities. Her philosophy is simple: people are basically good, well-intentioned, courageous, and able to learn, and her job is to provide a framework in which they can draw on their own inner resources to find creative solutions.

Leslie earned her master of science degree in organizational development at Case Western Reserve University after graduating cum laude from Wittenberg University with a bachelor of arts degree. She founded

Catalyst Consulting Group, Inc., in 1987, with the mission to build healthy and enduring organizations.

Her work in organizational development and change management has involved some of the nation's largest employers, including Chrysler Corporation and Ameritech Publishing; civic and community-service organizations, including United Way Services, the Child Life Council of America, and the American Red Cross; and organizations from the manufacturing, banking, health-care, and governmental sectors.

Leslie writes frequently for the *Cleveland Plain Dealer* and other publications, travels nationwide as a lecturer and keynote speaker, and has taught at John Carroll University and Baldwin Wallace College.

In those rare moments when she is not working, Leslie loves to travel to foreign lands. She has lived in England and Australia and once spent a year backpacking around the world. She has every intention of taking another major trip as soon as possible.

Leslie Yerkes can be contacted at:

Catalyst Consulting Group
1111 Chester Avenue
Cleveland, OH 44114
Tel: 216-241-3939
Fax: 216-241-3977

if you have fun ideas

I f you or anyone in your company has ideas or stories of successfully putting fun into your workplace, we would love to include them in future publications. Please mail, fax or email your ideas and stories to:

Business Outreach
c/o Fun at Work
1108 Chester Ave.
Cleveland, OH 44114
Fax: 216-348-0375
Email: hemsath@msn.com

Berrett-Koehler Publishers

BERRETT-KOEHLER is an independent publisher of books, periodicals, and other publications at the leading edge of new thinking and innovative practice on work, business, management, leadership, stewardship, career development, human resources, entrepreneurship, and global sustainability.

Since the company's founding in 1992, we have been committed to supporting the movement toward a more enlightened world of work by publishing books, periodicals, and other publications that help us to integrate our values with our work and work lives, and to create more humane and effective organizations.

We have chosen to focus on the areas of work, business, and organizations, because these are central elements in many people's lives today. Furthermore, the work world is going through tumultuous changes, from the decline of job security to the rise of new structures for organizing people and work. We believe that change is needed at all levels—individual, organizational, community, and global—and our publications address each of these levels.

We seek to create new lenses for understanding organizations, to legitimize topics that people care deeply about but that current business orthodoxy censors or considers secondary to bottom-line concerns, and to uncover new meaning, means, and ends for our work and work lives.

See next page for other books from Berrett-Koehler Publishers

Repacking Your Bags
Lighten Your Load for the Rest of Your Life

Richard J. Leider and David A. Shapiro

Learn how to climb out from under the many burdens you're carrying and find the fulfillment that's missing in your life. A simple yet elegant process teaches you to balance the demands of work, love, and place to create and live your own vision of success.

Paperback, 234 pages, 2/96 • ISBN 1-881052-87-7 CIP
Item no. 52877-189 $14.95

Hardcover, 1/95 • ISBN 1-881052-67-2 CIP • **Item no. 52672-189 $21.95**

Your Signature Path
Gaining New Perspectives on Life and Work

Geoffrey M. Bellman

Your Signature Path explores the uniqueness of the mark each of us makes in the world. Bellman offers thought-provoking insights and practical tools for evaluating who you are, what you are doing, and where you want your path to lead.

Hardcover, 200 pages, 10/96 • ISBN 1-57675-004-3 CIP
Item no. 50043-189 $24.95

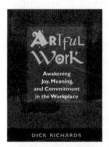

Artful Work
Awakening Joy, Meaning, and Commitment in the Workplace

Dick Richards

Dick Richards applies the assumptions of artists about work and life to the challenges facing people and organizations in today's rapidly changing world. He reminds us that all work can be artful, and that artfulness is the key to passion and commitment. Readers will learn to take an inspired approach to their work, renewing their experience of it as a creative, participative, and purposeful endeavor.

Hardcover, 144 pages, 3/95 • ISBN 1-881052-63-X CIP
Item no. 5263X-189 $25.00

Available at your favorite bookstore, or call (800) 929-2929

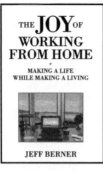

The Joy of Working from Home
Making a Life While Making a Living

Jeff Berner

D O YOU WORK at home, or just dream about it? Jeff Berner shows the current or prospective home-office worker how to set up an efficient home office and provides the support for making this major life change. Both pragmatic and inspiring, The Joy of Working at Home tells how to make a living and a life.

Paperback, 240 pages, 7/94 • ISBN - 1-881052-46-X CIP
Item no. 5246X-189 $12.95

The 4 Routes to Entrepreneurial Success

John B. Miner

J OHN MINER details four personality types that characterize successful entrepreneurs—Personal Achievers, Supersalespeople, Real Managers, and Expert Idea Generators—then shows you how to use this information to map out your own path to success.

Paperback, 280 pages, 9/96 • ISBN 1-881052-82-6 CIP •
Item no. 52826-189 $18.95

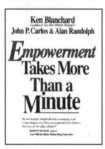

Empowerment Takes More than a Minute

Ken Blanchard, John Carlos, and Alan Randolph

E MPOWERMENT TAKES MORE THAN A MINUTE is the book that finally goes beyond the empowerment rhetoric to show managers how to achieve true, lasting results in their organizations. These expert authors explain how to empower the workforce by moving from a command-and-control mindset to a supportive, responsibility-centered environment in which all employees have the opportunity and responsibility to do their best. They explain how to build ownership and trust using three essential keys to making empowerment work in large and small organizations.

Hardcover, 140 pages, 12/96 • ISBN 1-881052-83-4 CIP
Item no. 52834-187 $20.00

Available at your favorite bookstore, or call (800) 929-2929